THE POSITIVE WORKBOOK

How you can do work you love

MIKE PEGG

ENHANCE LTD

Leamington Spa

First published in the United Kingdom in 1995 by
Enhance Ltd, The Hall, Radford Hall, Radford Semele,
Leamington Spa, CV31 1FH

British Library Cataloguing in Publication Data applied for.
ISBN 0-9521358-2-5

Design and origination by Magenta, Leamington Spa.
Printed and bound in Great Britain by Ebenezer Baylis, Worcester.

CONTENTS

Also by Mike Pegg:

Positive Leadership
The Positive Planet
The Art of Encouragement

INTRODUCTION

"WORK is love made visible," wrote Kahlil Gibran. Everybody is an artist, everybody is creative. Everybody can do work they enjoy; the art is getting somebody to pay you for doing it. This book focuses on how to follow your passions, be professional and achieve peak performance.

People who do work they love enjoy a gift for life. How do they find such a gift? They often learn from positive models, such as relatives, friends or famous people. Anita Roddick inspired budding entrepreneurs with her work at the Body Shop. Alec Dickson helped thousands of young people to find their vocations by creating Voluntary Service Overseas and Community Service Volunteers. Richard Bolles passed on wisdom to job-seekers by writing his classic *What Colour Is Your Parachute*? Success stories inspire people to start moving, but they must then tackle challenges in the real world. *Parachute* provided readers with practical tools they could use to build on their strengths, set specific goals and achieve ongoing success.

People often take three steps towards pursuing their vocation. They focus on their values, vision and visible results. They then perform creative work as architects, artists, business people, chefs, engineers, gardeners, nurses, painters, writers, or in their chosen profession. Soul wisdom is vital, but so is street wisdom. People need to get the right balance between pursuing their mission and paying their mortgage. *The Positive Workbook* explores how to make this happen. It shows how to clarify your values, translate these into a clear vision, and produce visible results.

Step One: Values

"Be true to yourself" is the guiding principle for people who do work they love. It sounds idealistic. How can you follow this path in a fast-changing commercial world? Chapter One provides practical tools and exercises which you can use:

- To clarify what is important to you in your life.
- To clarify your strengths.
- To clarify your best way of working.

It is vital to recognise where you work best: by yourself, in a team or an organisation, or as a leader. The next stage is to create a picture of the possible roads you can travel in your life.

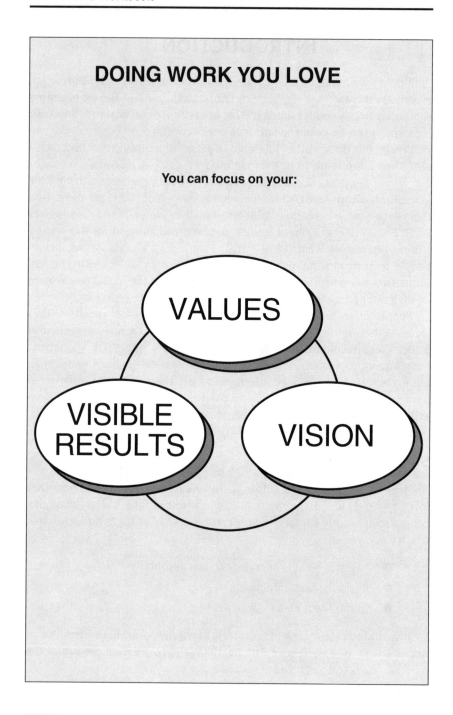

DOING WORK YOU LOVE

You can focus on your:

VALUES

VISIBLE RESULTS

VISION

Step Two: Vision

People who do work they love translate their values into a clear vision. They ask questions like: "What is the real mountain I want to climb in my life? How can I build on my outstanding talent? Who are my potential customers? How can I integrate what I want to offer with what my customers want? What is my strategy for reaching the mountain's summit?" Chapter Two provides practical tools and exercises which you can use:

- To clarify your goals.
- To clarify your strategy.
- To clarify the support you need to reach your goals.

Strategic thinking calls for recognising the pleasures and pains involved in pursuing your vision. Bearing in mind the pluses and minuses, ask yourself: "Am I serious? Am I prepared to accept the whole package?" If the answer is "Yes", the next stage is to make your vision happen.

Step Three: Visible Results

Peak Performers are good finishers. They dream, they do and they deliver. Finishing calls for more than having a vision; it calls for having superb implementation skills. It also calls for managing setbacks and finding creative solutions to problems. Chapter Three provides practical tools and exercises which you can use:

- To implement your strategy successfully.
- To do superb quality work.
- To encourage yourself, enjoy the journey and achieve your vision.

Finishing is another name for beginning. People who do work they enjoy believe in constant improvement and go on to tackle further challenges. Many pursue the path trodden by great teachers and pass on their wisdom to other people. The final chapter illustrates how you can share the fruits of your talent with future generations.

"What about developments in the world of work?" somebody may ask. "Don't rapid changes, such as technological revolutions, quickly make vocational books out of date?" It depends on the type of book. *Growing a*

Business by Paul Hawken, for example, shows that quality will always be in demand. Great teachers tell us that there are: a) Eternal things in life, and b) Evolving things in life. Timeless vocational books emphasise the eternal skills. Certain kinds of people will always find work — for example, those who are encouraging, enterprising and achieve excellence. *The Positive Workbook* focuses on such eternal skills and on applying them to doing work you love.

Creative thinking is vital in today's world, so two points are worth bearing in mind. First: People must develop both their inner qualities and their outer qualifications. Employers want staff who build on their strengths, manage change and finish successfully. Such qualities often take precedence over paper qualifications. Second: People can follow two roads towards reaching a goal; the conventional road and the creative road. The conventional road means following old systems. The creative road means asking: "What are the real results I want to achieve?" Keeping your eye on the vision, it calls for going around the system to reach your goals.

"How long will it take me to earn a living doing what I love?" many people ask. It depends on the person, their desire and their street wisdom. There are at least three approaches to making dreams happen: the "Sink or Swim" approach, the "Side-show" approach or the "Serious Plan" approach. My usual answer is: "Providing you keep doing the right thing in the right way every day, probably about three years. But you can also start tomorrow. Do what you love and get some successes in the next week." Three years sounds a long time, but it is better than slaving in the wrong job for the next 30 years.

How can you use this book? *The Positive Workbook* is, as its name implies, primarily a workbook. It contains exercises you can use by yourself, with your colleagues or with people who are seeking their vocation. Career Development workshops often begin by inviting people to clarify what they want to get from the programme. You can take a similar route by tackling the exercise on the following page called My Goals In Reading This Book. As I mentioned earlier, my aims are to offer a framework and practical tools which you can use:

- To do work you love.
- To help other people to do work they love.
- To act as course material on programmes designed to help people to find work they love.

MY GOALS IN
READING THIS BOOK

Write down three things you want to get from reading this book. For example: To do work you love, to help others to do work they love or to gather ideas to pass on to other people.

My goals in reading this book are:

●   To ....

       ....

       ....

●   To ....

       ....

       ....

●   To ....

       ....

       ....

The book is a resource bank. Sometimes you will find three, four or five exercises on the same theme. People are different, and offering choices means individuals are more likely to find exercises which are rewarding. You will also find some exercises from my other books. Why? I wanted to provide a comprehensive approach in one volume, rather than keep referring readers to exercises in *The Art of Encouragement*, *Positive Leadership* and *The Positive Planet*. Take the best and leave the rest.

The Positive Workbook gives one message which some readers may find surprising. People who do work they love are often quite "ordinary", but they develop good habits. They build on their strengths, set specific goals and achieve success. They offer the right "product" to the right customers at the right price in the right way. They get the right balance between creativity, customers and cash. Such simplicity is both inspiring and challenging. The hardest step is to develop the daily discipline of doing what works. Over the years, however, the discipline becomes part of your body as you get into the habit of expressing your talents.

"I keep coming back to the same answers, whichever exercises I try," said one person on a Career Development workshop. "What is the next step?" The good news was that the answers highlighted consistent truths in the person's life. The hard part was to translate their words into action. They chose to set reachable goals, get some early wins and build on their successes. Peak Performers go much further: they obsessively follow the truth about their talent and task in life. They then flow, focus and finish. Good luck and enjoy the journey towards doing work you love.

Step One:
VALUES

WHAT gets you out of bed in the morning? Your mission, your mortgage or a combination of both? Famous entrepreneurs are lauded in national newspapers, but most people who do work they enjoy never grab the headlines. Superstars can be inspiring, but onlookers can also feel paralysed, saying: "I can never be like Anita Roddick, Richard Branson or that new millionaire." Household names represent the tip of the iceberg, because there are thousands of ordinary people who do satisfying work every day. Providing you are willing to put in the effort, you can do work you love. You can also enjoy the fruits of your labours.

Doing work you enjoy is a habit. The more you do it, the easier it becomes, the more natural it becomes. "I began by doing what I enjoyed, which for me was making old-fashioned wooden tables and chairs," said Les, who runs a small carpentry business. How did he attract customers? "Our house faces a busy road, so I put tables and chairs on the lawn," he explained. "Drivers saw them as they drove past. People knocked on the door to ask the price, buy the goods or give special orders. My lawn is the shop window where I display window frames, wardrobes or whatever. I am now booked for two months ahead, but customers seem willing to wait." Les has tradeskills. He gets the right balance between being creative, getting customers and bringing in cash.

Where do you learn the habit of doing work you love? People learn from positive models: parents, teachers, relatives, friends, neighbours, heroes and heroines. The more models you have, the more choices you have, the more freedom you have. Success stories give you a glimpse of a different world. Scales fall from your eyes and, like the artist who mixes new colours on a palate, you see fresh possibilities. You start plotting new paths you can follow in your own life. Positive models are all around us, not just in magazines or on television. Here are a few relatively unknown people who make a living doing what they enjoy.

- Archie Duncanson is an American living in Sweden. Ten years ago he gave up his job as a computer programmer with Scandinavian Airlines and self-published a small book called *Ecology Begins At Home*. The book attracted national interest and led to his being invited to give lessons in schools and colleges. "I started each session by teaching people how to cook a saucepan full of spaghetti with a tablespoonful of water," he said. "They did not believe me, but I showed it was possible." Cooking and

PEOPLE NEED POSITIVE MODELS

People need positive models. The more models they have, the more choices they have, the more freedom they have. People can learn from their models and follow similar paths in their own way in their own lives.

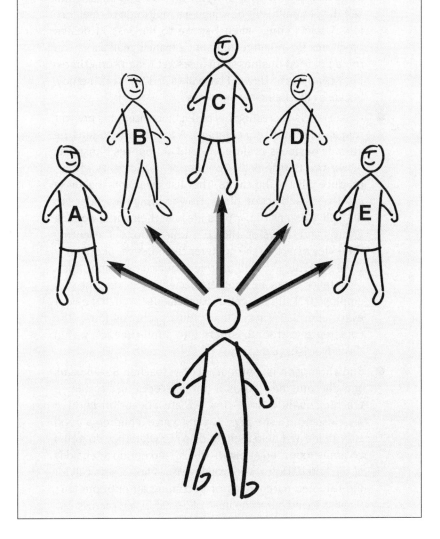

serving the spaghetti was interlaced with giving practical tips which people could use to live on much less energy. Archie now makes a living teaching people how to take care of their world by first taking care of their homes.

● Redundancy hurt Esther Moss when it arrived in her mid-forties. But she picked herself up and responded by becoming an inventor. She created, marketed and sold portable intensive care units for sick cats and dogs. "I still sell the pet units, but now juggle a multitude of freelance jobs," said Esther, when I spoke to her last. "I design brochures for Indian restaurants, organise mail shots and run a pet food business. Finances get tough sometimes, but I continue to thrive. I have always done work I enjoy, because I like being my own boss."

● Clive Francis is creating his perfect job within his present role at an advertising company. A former art student, he attends business conferences and announces himself as "Clive the Cartoonist". Conference participants always produce piles of flip charts. They list key points, business challenges and action plans. How to bring these ideas to life? Clive listens to people's ideas in their small working groups and draws on-the-spot illustrations. Presenting their views back to the conference audience, people use Clive's pictures to add a professional dimension. Post-conference packs are another speciality. Why does he stay employed? "I still like getting the cheque through the door every month," says Clive. "But I am building the conference cartoon business into a full-time job within the advertising company."

● Sue Thompson is a primary school teacher. Seven years ago she quit her job as a hotel receptionist to take a teaching qualification. "Now I create a beautiful world in my classroom," she says. "I aim to give children a good start in life and help them to discover what they do well. I go home refreshed at night, which I did not do after a day at the hotel." Doing work you love does not always call for life-threatening changes or becoming an entrepreneur. Sue has found her niche in an old-established profession.

● Nicholas Albery is a pioneer who publicises ideas for improving the quality of life. He founded the Institute for Social Inventions in London, which is backed by sponsors such as The Rowntree Trust. Hundreds of caring, creative and sometimes crazy ideas can be found in his giant volume *The Book of Visions*, which was published by Virgin. The UK Institute runs an annual competition for social inventions, with cash prizes for the winners, and Nicholas conducts Social Invention workshops throughout Europe. He makes his living by helping to build a better world.

People often take three steps towards making dreams happen. They dream, they do and they deliver. Where do they get the power to follow their calling? Everybody has a track record of achievement, starting with their struggle to be born. Try tackling the exercise called Being True To Yourself. Describe a time in your life when you successfully did something you believed in. You may have followed a dream, fought for a principle or achieved some other goal. Describe five things you did right and how you can take similar paths in the future. Everybody has successful patterns which they can pursue to shape their destiny.

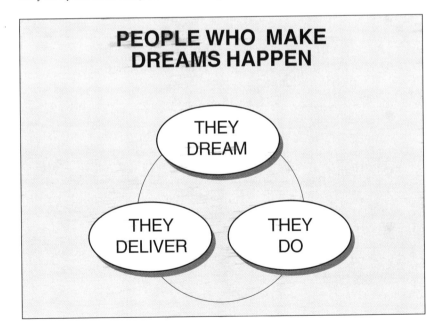

BEING TRUE TO YOURSELF

a) Describe a time in your life when you did something that you believed in and felt you were successful.

● When I _____

_____

b) What were you doing right then? Write five things you did right to accomplish what you believed in.

● I _____

● I _____

● I _____

● I _____

● I _____

c) Describe specific things you can do to follow these paths again in the future.

● I can _____

_____

● I can _____

_____

● I can _____

_____

How do you embark on the road to doing work you love? People normally pursue one of three routes. They follow the "Sink or Swim", "Side-show" or "Serious Plan" approach. Let's explore the pluses and minuses of travelling each of these routes. "

● The "Sink or Swim" approach

"I am totally fed up with my present job," somebody may say. "I will hand in my notice on Friday, give up everything and start afresh. I will make it or bust." Sounds brave and sometimes it works. Penniless emigrants left forbidding shores to amass fortunes in America. But there are also risks. The pluses of this approach include: you start straight away; you are forced to use your creativity; you feel great if you succeed. The minuses include: you have little security; you have few customers; you use all your energy to survive.

● The "Side-show" approach

"I will keep my full-time office job and run my hairdressing business in the evenings and weekends," somebody may say. "If the part-time business takes off, I will quit my present job. I will invest the time and money needed to turn the hairdressing into a profitable business." The pluses of this approach include: you keep your sense of security; you build from a position of strength; you create a network of customers that provides the foundation for building your business. The minuses include: you will feel split and exhausted; you may never progress beyond the business being a hobby; you must still take calculated risks when you go full-time.

● The "Serious Plan" approach

"I will stay in my present job for the moment," somebody may say, "but aim to become a self-employed training consultant in 18 months' time. By this date I must have customer orders which will eventually earn £30,000 per year. Starting from this destination and working backwards, I will make a serious plan showing the practical things I must do to translate the dream into reality. Providing I implement this plan every day, I will reach my goal by this date."

The pluses include: you keep your present financial security; you build from strength; you start work on achieving your dream; you minimise the risks; you reach satisfying milestones along the road; you create the basis for a successful business. The minuses include: you must discipline yourself to implement your plan; you will experience conflicts of interest, especially with present customers you want to carry over into your new business; you will never feel 100 per cent certain you have financial security.

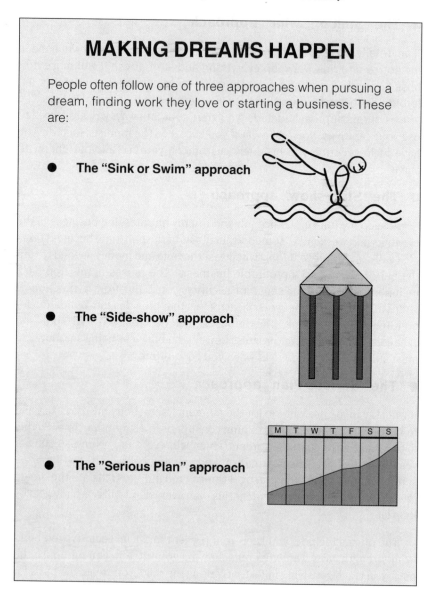

MAKING DREAMS HAPPEN

People often follow one of three approaches when pursuing a dream, finding work they love or starting a business. These are:

- **The "Sink or Swim" approach**

- **The "Side-show" approach**

- **The "Serious Plan" approach**

What is the best approach? Much depends on your view of the pluses and minuses. Successful entrepreneurs build from strength. They offer the right product to the right people at the right price in the right way. Mythology says that entrepreneurs take risks, but they often take only calculated risks. Pioneers feel it would be a greater risk for them not to take the risk. Why? They would regret missing a golden opportunity and feel unhappy about not realising a dream.

Entrepreneurs anticipate the pleasures and pains, but feel able to manage the setbacks. Some analysis is vital for plotting the route, but too much can create paralysis. Looking back over the years, one business owner reflected: "Sometimes it is best not to know everything that can go wrong. If you worry about every conceivable disaster, you will never do anything in life." Let's explore what generates the power for people to pursue their calling.

YOU CAN DO WORK
YOU BELIEVE IN

David Grubb, the Director of Feed The Children, is a belief-driven person. He highlights the power of belief when speaking about the agency's work across the world. "Some people don't understand that we must provide the right food for each ethnic group plagued by hunger. Potential donors sometimes argue: 'If a person is at death's door, they will eat anything.' This is just the time when people who hold certain beliefs will *not* eat food which is against their religion. Belief to them is stronger than life itself."

Belief shapes our attitudes to life and death. It also generates energy to pursue our chosen calling. People use different names to describe their jobs. They may call it a mission, a purpose or a vocation. What puts a spring into your step as you walk to work in the morning? The following pages provide several exercises on the theme of beliefs. These approach the same subject from different angles, so sometimes they overlap. "Values" means more to some people, for example, than does "Philosophy". Treat the exercises as a menu. Tackle those that mean something to you.

● My values

What are your three key values? One person on a Career Development workshop wrote: "My values are: 1) To care for my family. 2) To care for other people. 3) To care for the planet." Later we will be exploring how you can translate your values into a clear vision and produce visible results.

● My beliefs

Write three things you believe in. These can be about life, work, the spirit or whatever. For example, I believe that: 1) People can be positive. 2) People can do positive work. 3) People can build a positive planet. What are your beliefs?

● My life philosophy

Describe your life philosophy. While similar to the values and beliefs exercises, you may wish to expand on these themes and describe the things you want out of life. People choose different ways to describe their life philosophy, so write it in your own way.

● My valuables

Write or draw the things that are really valuable to you in your life. One person wrote: "My valuables are my wife; our children; our house; our pets; my health; my ability to paint; my customers, the people who pay our bills." What is valuable to you in your life?

● My positive models

Seeing is believing. If you see something is possible, you believe it is possible. Write the names of three people who you believe have done work they loved. Describe five things they did right and how you can follow similar paths to do work you love in your own life.

● My perfect work

What would be your ideal work? Begin by describing or drawing your perfect job. How can you find or create this kind of job? Complete the exercise by describing the specific steps you can take to find your perfect work.

● My commitment

Encouragers do what they can do, rather than talk about what they can't do. Write two lists. First: What you can do in your life. Second: What you can't do in your life. One person wrote: "I can encourage my child; teach inspiring lessons at school; tackle problems I can solve. I can't give unlimited time to everybody; persuade people to change; right every wrong in the world."

MY VALUES

Describe your key values in life. One person on a Career Development workshop wrote: "My values are: 1) To care for my family. 2) To care for other people. 3) To care for the planet." What are your values?

My key values are:

● ....

....

....

● ....

....

....

● ....

....

....

MY BELIEFS

Write three things you believe in. These can be in any area; for example, the things you believe in about life, work, the spirit or whatever.

I believe:

1) ....

....

....

....

2) ....

....

....

....

3) ....

....

....

....

MY LIFE PHILOSOPHY

Try writing down your life-philosophy. There are many ways to do this, so write it in your own way. For example: You might describe your values, beliefs or what you want to do in your life.

My life-philosophy Is:

●
....
....
....

●
....
....
....

●
....
....
....

●
....
....
....

MY VALUABLES

Write down or draw the things that are really valuable to you in your life.

The things that are really valuable to me in my life are:

MY POSITIVE MODELS

a) Write the names of three people who you believe have done work they loved.

- ....
- ....
- ....

b) Write five things you believe they did right to accomplish work they loved.

- They ....
- They ....
- They ....
- They ....
- They ....

c) Describe three things you can do to follow these steps in your own way to accomplish work you love.

- I can ....
- I can ....
- I can ....

MY PERFECT WORK

What would be your ideal work? Describe or draw your perfect job and then write steps you can take to make this happen.

My perfect work would be:

- ....
  ....

- ....
  ....

- ....
  ....

The concrete steps I can take towards creating my perfect work are:

- ....
  ....

- ....
  ....

- ....
  ....

MY COMMITMENT

What I can do in my life:

1) I can ....

2) I can ....

3) I can ....

4) I can ....

5) I can ....

What I can't do in my life:

1) I can't ....

2) I can't ....

3) I can't ....

You can get the right balance between your mission and mortgage

People choose different routes to happiness. Caitlin Allen earned a first-class degree with a distinction, gaining an A in every subject. While studying at university, she also plunged herself into voluntary work and edited my book *The Positive Planet*. A multi-talented person, the commercial world lay at her feet, but she opted for a low-paid job assisting homeless people in Edinburgh. "It is simply what I want to do," she says. Like an increasing number of values-driven young people, Caitlin is pursuing her chosen road, rather than borrowing from banks or incurring crippling debts for life. Before exploring this theme further, you may wish to read the old story called *The Contented Fisherman*.

THE CONTENTED FISHERMAN

The Southern fisherman had completed his work for the day and was sitting on the beach. The rich industrialist from the North was horrified to find him lying lazily beside his boat, enjoying the sunset.

"Why aren't you out fishing?" asked the industrialist.

"Because I have caught enough fish for one day," said the fisherman.

"Why don't you catch more than you need?" said the industrialist.

"What could I do with them?" asked the fisherman.

"You could earn more money," was the reply. "With the cash you could have a motor fixed to your boat. Then you could go into deeper waters, catch more fish and make enough money to buy nylon nets. These would bring you more fish and more money. Soon you would have enough money to own two boats. Then you could create a large fleet, sell it off and make lots of money."

"What would I do then?" asked the fisherman.

"Then you could sit down and enjoy life," said the industrialist.

"What do you think I am doing now?" said the contented fisherman.

"The fisherman's story sounds attractive, but I must earn money," somebody may argue. "I must buy food, clothe the kids and pay the electricity bill." People often take on debts in their twenties and fail to escape from the financial prison. Some feel satisfied gathering possessions, but others experience pain. Waking up one morning, they ask themselves: "What do I want out of life? How can I care for my loved ones? How can I do these things in a positive way?" Miracles seldom occur overnight but, providing people are willing to change their lifestyle, it is possible to find solutions. How to make this happen? One way to start is by tackling the next exercise.

● My mission and mortgage

Many people face the challenge of pursuing their mission and paying their mortgage. Write three lists. First: How you can pursue your mission in life. Second: How you can pay your mortgage. Third: How you can get the right balance between your mission and mortgage. Some ideas may spring to mind straight away, others may arrive when reading the following chapters. So you may wish to return to this exercise after completing the book.

People follow the mission road, the mortgage road or a combination of both. They experience pleasures and pains whichever road they pursue. People such as Frank Lloyd Wright, Alexander Calder and Mozart were big artists. Many of us are small artists. We can still give the fruits of our talent to the world, however, providing we build on our strengths.

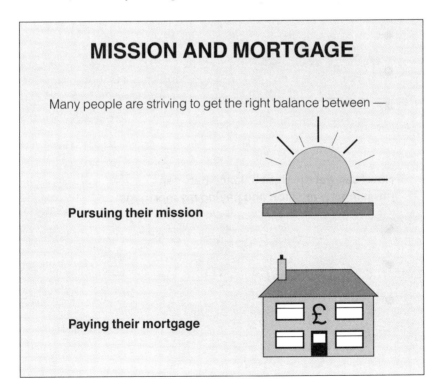

MISSION AND MORTGAGE

Many people are striving to get the right balance between —

Pursuing their mission

Paying their mortgage

MISSION AND MORTGAGE

How I can pursue my mission:

- ....
- ....
- ....

How I can pay my mortgage:

- ....
- ....
- ....

How I can get the right balance between pursuing my mission and paying my mortgage:

- ....
- ....
- ....

YOU CAN BUILD
ON YOUR STRENGTHS

Micke Larsson was 17 when I met him on a one-day course for unemployed young people in Northern Sweden. My brief was simple: "Do something to help them increase their self-confidence and to find work." The teenagers responded well and, after an hour, I asked each person to draw a poster headed My Ideal Life. Coffee time arrived and they filed out to take a break. Returning to the main hall, I discovered Micke scaling a vertical wall. "I enjoy climbing," he explained, as he walked across a narrow beam. "Look at my poster. It shows what I plan to do in my life."

Labelled a failure at school, Micke had drawn a picture of himself climbing a mountain in Jämtland, Sweden. At the foot of the mountain was a small cabin, with a woman and child standing nearby. "My ideal life would be to earn my living climbing," he said. "Leading tourists across the mountains is a seasonal job, so I must find some other way of getting money. I also want to get married and have children." Fire burned behind Micke's eyes as he spoke. The door was flung open by people returning from coffee and we continued the workshop.

Two months later I received a newspaper photograph showing Micke hanging on a rope suspended from the top of a church tower. The article reported that he had started a company called "High Service". Carrying his mountaineering equipment from village to village, he specialised in cleaning church spires. Marketing was deceptively simple. The local newspaper invariably publicised how he had created his own job during Sweden's toughest recession. He copied the article, sent it to the next village and asked if they wanted him to clean their church. Several more articles followed in the next months, but then I lost track of Micke.

Ten years later I returned to Sweden to run a workshop in Uppsala. Two young people introduced themselves at the start of the programme. "We come from a company which makes safety equipment for fire-fighters, steeplejacks and other people who work at height," they said. Based in Jämtland, the company exported quality products throughout Europe. The owner was Micke Larsson, who was married with children. They spoke passionately about their radical safety designs and I recalled the morning I found the "school failure" climbing the wall. Not everybody has Micke's drive, but he demonstrates the power of building on your talents.

How can you tap your creativity? One way is to do what you enjoy.

Creative people find it hard to distinguish between play and work. They get involved in "serious play", becoming so absorbed in an activity that they are oblivious to time. What are your passions? When do you feel most alive? What are your strengths? Try tackling the exercises below which focus on your creativity. We will then explore how you can earn money doing some of the things you love.

● Thirty things I enjoy doing

The key to your talents is found in doing what you enjoy. One person began his list by writing: "I enjoy: gardening; growing vegetables; cooking; organising the local fête; flying in balloons; walking in the woods; writing about nature; helping people to be happy; etc." Describe 30 things you enjoy doing.

● My passions

Passion is an even stronger feeling than enjoyment. One person began his list by writing: "My passions are: providing for my family; educating dyslexic children; rebuilding old cars; playing the drums; supporting Norwich City; protecting the countryside; etc." What are your passions?

● When do I feel most creative?

What part does creativity play in your life? Some people perform their daily work and integrate creativity into this work. Other people make creativity the central theme and weave their work around this drive. One person wrote: "I feel most creative when I am working with my Apple Macintosh; I am writing about nature; I am walking in the forest; I am trying to find solutions to problems; etc." You can then explore how to weave work around some of the creative themes in your life.

● A sense of play

"There is nothing more serious than play," somebody once said. Alexander Calder, the inventor of the mobile, for example, found it hard to distinguish between play and work. When do you feel totally absorbed in your work? When do the hours pass without your noticing the clock? Describe the times when you experience a sense of play, serious or otherwise, in your work. For example: when solving a problem; when designing a dress; when writing an article; etc.

● My strengths

Quality is something people will always buy, even in a recession. What do you do best? Brainstorm the things you do well — these can be big or small things — then list your top three qualities. As with all these exercises, it is then important to explore how you can make money pursuing some of the activities in which you perform outstanding work.

THIRTY THINGS I ENJOY DOING

Write a list of things you enjoy doing. For example: dancing; travelling; spending time with grandchildren; helping people; playing with computers; climbing mountains; etc.

I enjoy:

* .... * ....

* .... * ....

* .... * ....

* .... * ....

* .... * ....

* .... * ....

* .... * ....

* .... * ....

* .... * ....

* .... * ....

* .... * ....

* .... * ....

* .... * ....

* .... * ....

* .... * ....

MY PASSIONS

Describe your passions. For example: caring for your family; gardening; playing music; weaving; teaching young children; etc.

My passions are:

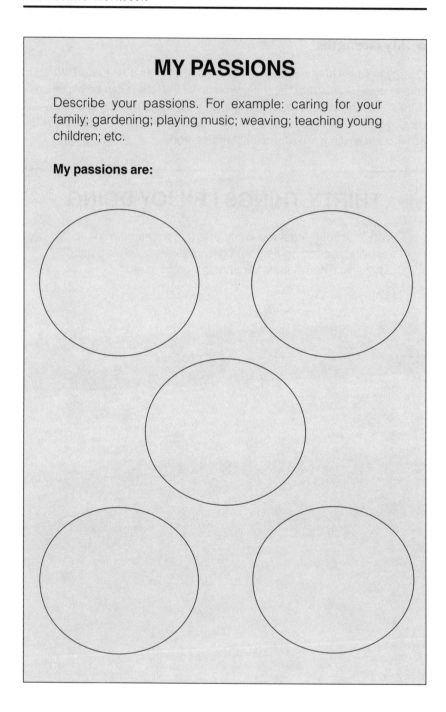

WHEN DO I FEEL MOST CREATIVE?

Describe the times you feel most creative. For example: writing; walking in the woods; sailing; working alone; painting pictures; listening to music; etc.

I feel most creative when:

- I ....
- I ....
- I ....
- I ....
- I ....
- I ....
- I ....
- I ....
- I ....
- I ....

A SENSE OF PLAY

There is nothing more serious than play. Describe when you experience a sense of play in your work. For example: when solving a problem; when teaching a class; when designing a dress; etc.

The times I experience a sense of play are:

● When

● When

● When

● When

● When

● When

MY STRENGTHS

Brainstorm the things you do well — these can be big or small things — then list your top three qualities. Follow this by brainstorming and then clarifying ways you can earn money doing some of these things.

My strengths are:

1) ....
....

2) ....
....

3) ....
....

How I can earn money doing some of these things:

1) ....
....

2) ....
....

3) ....
....

You can clarify how to earn money doing what you love

"My work is teaching children to play the violin, but their learning process goes much deeper," says Tamara Himmelstrand. "Playing music is a way they can share their inner beauty. Getting success helps them to gain a sense of peace. Children and parents see they have inner treasures and can gain satisfaction by nurturing what they have within, rather than by constantly looking for outside assurance. Educating children is rewarding. Early success can provide the foundation for shaping their future lives."

Tamara's words sounds idealistic, but she also has tradeskills. Trained by Yehudi Menuhin, she obtained a part-time job at a music school for children. Tuition methods at the school tended to be mechanistic. Pupils learned to play correctly but without sparkle. Tamara's approach upset the teachers but delighted the parents. Focusing on the basics, she encouraged children to enjoy the music and express their personalities. Parents saw the results at concerts. Tamara was plied with requests for extra private tuition, which formed the basis for starting her own business. Going "legitimate" was the hardest step. Paying tax meant charging parents double the fee they paid to the school. Music created by her pupils convinced them, however, and Tamara now has a flourishing practice.

People often pursue a deceptively simple-looking route towards doing work they love. Tamara Himmelstrand focused on helping children to play the violin; Micke Larsson focused on climbing; Caitlin Allen focused on assisting homeless people; Archie Duncanson focused on ecology; Anita Roddick focused on selling "cosmetics without cruelty". Such people often use the three keywords for being creative, "What? How? When?", to plot the route towards doing satisfying work. You can navigate your own path by asking :

    a)   What do I enjoy doing?

    b)   How can I make money doing some of these things?

    c)   When do I want to begin?

Creative thinking is needed to tackle these challenges. Imagine you are running a workshop on Career Development. The aim is to help people to find or create work they love, either inside or outside an organisation. How can you encourage people to think outside present parameters and use their imagination? One approach is to use the next exercise. It provides a vehicle for people helping each other to develop new careers.

Start by asking each person to make a poster headed "Thirty Things I Enjoy Doing." Then invite people to form groups, find a place to talk and share their lists. One person then volunteers to explore his or her future possibilities. People focus on how the volunteer can earn money doing what he or she enjoys. (The poster serves as a starting point. It is rewarding to invite the volunteer to elaborate on what has been written.) People can brainstorm, act as consultants, advisors, marketers or play any other role which helps the volunteer to achieve his or her goal. Forty-five minutes later the group returns to the main room. They present posters showing how the volunteer can earn money doing what he or she enjoys. Discussions then spark off other ideas which people can use to find rewarding work. Two themes often emerge during these presentations.

First: People need even more positive models. Writing in his book *Zen in the Art of Making a Living*, Laurence G. Boldt lists over 300 businesses people can start with little or no money. Some examples: aerobic instructor; auctioneer; curriculum vitae service; electrician; gardener; interior designer; pet sitting; translation service. (Further examples are given on the following pages.) Sometimes it is helpful to show people this list before they embark on the exercise. It speeds up the process of helping the volunteer to earn money doing what he or she loves.

Second: People need even greater practice at thinking outside conventional parameters. Many volunteers write, for example, that they enjoy helping people. Groups then normally suggest that the person becomes a teacher, a social worker or join some other old-established profession. While this may be the best solution, it is valuable to find the person's real niche. What type of people do they like meeting: children, teenagers, parents, students, alcoholics, business directors? What gives them a buzz when helping people: listening, teaching a skill, solving a problem or some other activity? What is their outstanding talent? How can they use this gift to help people?

During the past 30 years, for example, I have been fortunate enough to be employed as an Encourager. My preferred niche is to offer practical tools which people can use to encourage themselves and other people. It is also to offer a framework which they can use to do three things. First: to be positive. Second: to do positive work. Third: to build a positive planet. How do you earn money as an Encourager? Employers in social work, education, sports and business have provided the financial backing over the years. (I redefine these employers as "sponsors".) Some of these jobs are shown on page 43. Other people would choose other jobs as a way of expressing this particular life-theme.

GROUP EXERCISE:
Helping a person to earn money doing what he or she enjoys

1) Each person begins by writing a list of what they enjoy doing. People then form groups and go through the following process.

2) The people share their lists of what they enjoy doing. The group then asks for a volunteer who wants to look at how he can earn money doing what he enjoys.

3) The group's task is to focus on one or more of the things that the person enjoys doing. The goal is for them to return to the big group with a poster which outlines the things the person can do to earn money doing what he enjoys. The group members can brainstorm, act as consultants, advisors, marketers or play any other role which helps them to achieve the goal.

4) Each group presents back two posters to the big group (see below).

WHAT THE PERSON ENJOYS DOING	HOW THE PERSON CAN EARN MONEY DOING SOME OF THESE THINGS
• _____	• _____
• _____	• _____
• _____	• _____
• _____	• _____
• _____	• _____

BUSINESSES YOU CAN START WITH LITTLE MONEY

Writing in his book *Zen in the Art of Making a Living,* Laurence G. Boldt lists over 300 businesses that can be started with little or no money. Here are some he mentions:

*	Accountancy	*	Aerobic instructor
*	Auctioneer	*	Beautician
*	Bed and breakfast	*	Bicycle repair
*	CV service	*	Car cleaning
*	Care of animals	*	Cartoonist
*	Clown	*	Computer consultant
*	Dance instructor	*	Desktop publishing
*	Drywalling	*	Electrician
*	Etiquette training	*	Event planning
*	Flower selling	*	Furniture making
*	Gardener	*	Graphic design
*	Gutter cleaning	*	Handyman service
*	House cleaning	*	House painting
*	Ice-cream seller	*	Image consultant
*	Interior design	*	Jewellery design

* Jewellery repair
* Juggler
* Knife sharpening
* Knitting
* Landscaping
* Limo service
* Lunch delivery service
* Marketing consultant
* Mobile disc jockey
* Mobile hairdresser
* Nail salon
* Nanny placement
* Newsletter compilation
* Outdoor guide
* Outdoor maintenance
* Pet sitting
* Photographer
* Pottery
* Recycling service
* Retailing with a cart
* Roof restoration
* Shoe repair
* Second-hand bookshop
* Second-hand clothes selling
* Stand-up comedian
* Tax service
* Translation service
* Typing service
* Upholstery cleaning
* Upholstery repair
* Used car inspections
* VCR installation
* Vending machine work
* Wallpaper hanging
* Window cleaning
* Word processing
* Writing service
* Yoga instructor

Some of the ways in which I have earned money as an encourager are:

* Being a housefather for mentally-handicapped children.

* Running therapeutic communities for teenagers, drug addicts and former mental patients.

* Teaching family therapy.

* Running courses on Encouragement, Creativity, Career Development, Positive Leadership, Peak Performance and Senior Team Development.

* Writing, publishing and marketing books about encouragement.

* Designing distance-learning materials.

* Designing training programmes for organisations.

* Being a Youth Development Officer for a professional football team and acting as a consultant to sports teams.

* Being a strategic consultant to senior teams in the public and private sector.

* Being a company coach and acting as a "Third Ear" for chief executives.

* Giving keynote speeches at conferences.

* Going back to my roots and encouraging people to find or do work they love.

What is your life-theme? What do you want to offer to people? What will be the benefits to your potential customers? Everybody is good at something, but it can take years of exploration to find your outstanding talent. It is also important to clarify where you work best, which is another step taken by people who do work they love.

You can choose your best way to work

People are different. People have different bodies, eyes, hair, talents, interests and hopes. They also have different ways of working. Archie Duncanson prefers to work alone for much of the time, but then emerges to share his know-how with the world. Clive Francis, the cartoonist, prefers to work in a small team or an organisation. Anita Roddick prefers to work as a leader. Different flowers blossom in different climates; different people blossom in different situations. People need to find the right environment to make the best use of their talents. What is your best way of working?

You can take a step towards finding out by tackling the three following exercises. Begin by doing the exercise that appeals to you immediately. Follow this by tackling your second and third choices. We will then explore the skills needed to travel along the different roads towards producing creative work.

● My creative times by myself

Describe a time in your life when you did creative work by yourself. For example: When you built a boat, wrote a book or achieved some other goal. Continue the exercise by describing five things you did right to do creative work by yourself. Conclude by writing three things you can do to follow similar paths to perform creative work by yourself in the future.

● My creative times in a team

Describe a time when you did creative work as part of a team in the arts, business or any walk of life. (If you prefer, you can describe a time when you did creative work in an organisation.) For example: When you played your part in a theatre troupe, choral society or project group in a company. Continue by describing five things you did right as a team member. Conclude by writing three things you can do to perform creative work in a team in the future.

● My creative times as a leader

Describe a time when you did creative work as a leader in the arts, business or any walk of life. For example: When you led a voluntary group, sports team or sales department in a company. Continue by describing five things you did right as a leader to encourage people to do their best. Conclude by writing three things you can do to perform creative work as a leader in the future.

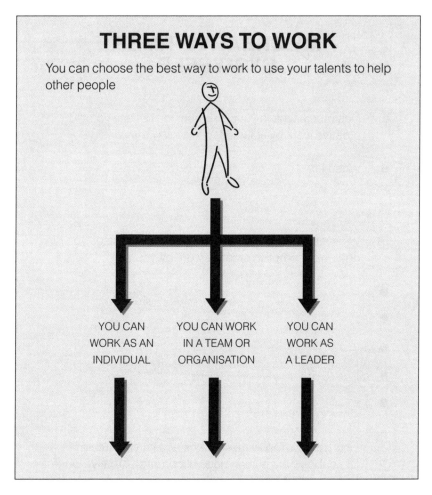

THREE WAYS TO WORK

You can choose the best way to work to use your talents to help other people

YOU CAN WORK AS AN INDIVIDUAL

YOU CAN WORK IN A TEAM OR ORGANISATION

YOU CAN WORK AS A LEADER

Sometimes you may switch between the three different roads. Tamara Himmelstrand, for example, spends hours alone practising the violin and designing lessons. In addition to her one-to-one sessions with pupils, she co-teaches courses with her husband, Jonas, which calls for teamwork. Employing her music-making as a metaphor, Tamara also leads coaching courses for business people, showing how to encourage staff to do their best. She agrees the course agenda, inspires people to want to reach the goals, and guides them to achieving success. People may pursue all three roads, but they frequently return to their preferred method for performing creative work.

MY CREATIVE TIMES
BY MYSELF

a) Describe a time in your life when you believe you did creative work by yourself.

● When I
....

....

b) What were you doing right then? Write five things you did right to accomplish creative work by yourself.

● I
....

● I
....

● I
....

● I
....

● I
....

c) How can you follow these paths again in the future? Describe what you can do to accomplish creative work by yourself.

● I can
....

● I can
....

● I can
....

MY CREATIVE TIMES
IN A TEAM

a) Describe a time in your life when you believe you did creative work working as part of a team or, if you wish, as part of an organisation.

● When I ....

   ....

b) What were you doing right then? Write five things you did right to do creative work as part of the team.

● I ....

● I ....

● I ....

● I ....

● I ....

c) How can you follow these paths again in the future? Describe what you can do to perform creative work·as part of a team.

● I can ....

● I can ....

● I can ....

MY CREATIVE TIMES
AS A LEADER

a) Describe a time in your life when you believe you did creative work as a leader.

● When I ....
....

b) What were you doing right then? Write five things you did right to do creative work as a leader and encourage people to do their best.

● I ....

● I ....

● I ....

● I ....

● I ....

c) How can you follow these paths again in the future? Describe what you can do to perform creative work as a leader.

● I can ....

● I can ....

● I can ....

You can work by yourself

"Think like an immigrant", is the common advice to people who run their own businesses, whether they are artists, window-cleaners, consultants or whatever. They must be hungry, ready to sweat and prepared to think outside conventional rules. Artists sometimes find a "sponsor" who provides protection and money that frees them to pursue their craft. Can you find a "sponsor"? If not, you must develop the qualities demonstrated by successful entrepreneurs: Talent, Tenacity and Tradeskills.

TALENT

Twenty years ago I had the opportunity to sit in on several lessons given by an English teacher called Joan, who taught Creative Writing courses at Antioch College in Ohio. She began her first session with new students by announcing: "Welcome to the class. You all have talent. If you have one talent, you are lucky. If you have ten talents, you are in trouble. You may spend years agonising over which talent to use in your life." Sometimes it is better to have one small talent, rather than to be multi-talented.

Everybody is good at something, the hard part is to identify and nurture this ability to fruition. The first step is to identify what you do best. The second step is to build on your strength, to set clear goals and to do good quality work. The third step is to commit yourself to constant improvement and continually perform outstanding work. You may wish to tackle the exercise called The Entrepreneurial Test. Start with the first part which focuses on talent. How do you rate your own ability to perform superb quality work in a particular field? On a scale 0—10, how would rate yourself in terms of talent?

TENACITY

"Potential is easy to find," Joan continued, when introducing the Creative Writing course to her students. "I see ability all the time with young people in the arts. Dancers, writers and actors are ten a penny. The question is: Are you prepared to labour? If you aren't, that's fine, but you must then see writing as a hobby. If you want to produce books, you must be ready to toil for the next 50 years."

Genius, we are told, calls for 10 per cent inspiration and 90 per cent perspiration. Running your own business calls for being willing to set specific goals, sweat and overcome setbacks. Problems are an everyday factor of business life. Successful entrepreneurs are like peak performers, however. They show great strength when tackling challenges. They use setbacks as the springboard to greater achievements and make a habit of finishing things. How do you rate your own ability to keep working hard? On a scale 0—10, how would rate yourself in terms of tenacity?

TRADESKILLS

Tradeskills call for street wisdom. People with such skills have a nose for the market. They like contacting customers, selling their services, talking about

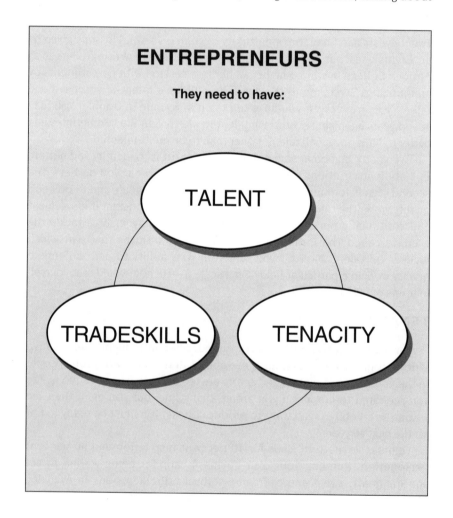

money, creating a healthy profit and building a business. They happily accept the highs and lows of entrepreneurial life. Other people find the trading process difficult or distasteful. Running a business calls for developing tradeskills, otherwise you go bankrupt. But do the same rules apply to other fields?

Eric Maisel's book, *Staying Sane In The Arts*, explains how learning such skills can earn money from painting, dancing or acting. How can you finance your art? Taking the case of the painter, Eric writes:

"There are essentially seven sources of income available to you as an artist. You may want to treat them as if they make up a buffet meal from which you select according to what's available and most palatable. These seven sources are:

1. Art products and performances.
2. Commercial products (including commissions, genre work, commercials).
3. Grants, residencies, gallery stipends.
4. Related careers (including tutoring, producing, agenting, editing, doing art therapy).
5. Unrelated day jobs.
6. Income from a mate or spouse.
7. Income from family and friends."

You may prefer to focus on art products and performances, writes Eric, but this seldom offers the most plentiful source of money. Artists throughout history have demonstrated the ability to juggle their jobs. Perfect solutions are rare. You may need to put together a financial programme which ensures you eat and offers maximum freedom to pursue your art.

Tradeskills are required to make money. What if you don't possess such skills? You have three options. First: Find some other form of "sponsorship". Choose an easier life than running a business. Second: Develop such skills. Although this is possible, such attempts often result in failure, because tradeskills are learned early in life. Third: Build on your strengths, earn more money and hire people with complementary skills. On a scale 0—10, how would you rate yourself in terms of tradeskills? Running a company does not appeal to everybody, so let's explore the next road people take towards performing creative work.

THE ENTREPRENEURIAL TEST

People need to have certain qualities to succeed as entrepreneurs. They need to have talent, tenacity and tradeskills. Rate yourself in each of these areas on a scale 0—10.

● TALENT

The ability to perform superb quality work in a particular field. Remember it is better to have one talent which you develop, rather than ten talents which you neglect. On a scale 0—10, how would you rate yourself in terms of talent?

● TENACITY

The ability to focus, work hard and finish things. You also need to be able to oversome setbacks. On a scale 0—10, how would you rate yourself in terms of tenacity?

● TRADESKILLS

The ability to sell your service, make healthy profits, build a business and accept the pluses and minuses of entrepreneurial life. If you don't have these skills, it will be important to find somebody who does. On a scale 0—10, how would you rate yourself in terms of tradeskills?

You can work in a team or in an organisation

"Teamwork gives me a buzz," somebody may say. "I like working with people. The social contact and support inspires me to do my best. Pooling our strengths to reach a specific target gives me a sense of pride and achievement."

Teamwork can be exciting, but bear three points in mind before applying to join any team or organisation. First: It must be one where you agree with its values, vision and visible results. Second: It must be one which has the right people implementing the right strategy in the right way. Third: It must be one where you can build on your strengths and make a positive contribution. Providing the answer to all three questions is "Yes", you have the foundation for achieving success.

Job interviews are a two-way process in the modern world. You look for certain qualities in a workplace, but are you marketable? There are: a) Eternal things in life, and b) Evolving things in life. Certain kinds of people will always find work; those who are encouraging, enterprising and achieve excellence. My Employability is an exercise which people do when attending workshops on Career Development. Tackle it to see if you have the qualities desired by modern employers.

BEING AN ENCOURAGER

Encouragers are attractive to potential employers. Why? They have a good attitude and contribute to the culture. Successful teams are in a buyer's market and can afford to be selective. They do not waste energy "persuading" people to adopt certain beliefs or behaviour. They look for people who have the following qualities:

- People who take responsibility.
- People who have a positive attitude.
- People who are good team members.
- People who are good people-managers.
- People who make a positive contribution to both the culture and the bottom line.

Sounds a demanding list, but it is a good starting point. Negative people upset colleagues and customers, creating problems which can prove costly. Technical skill is invaluable, but so are people-skills. On a scale 0—10, how do you rate yourself as an Encourager?

BEING ENTERPRISING

Enterprising people are attractive to employers. Flat organisations demand that staff make decisions at the closest point to the customer. People no longer have time to write a memo and wait for management approval. They must take immediate action at the hotel reception desk, the airline check-in or the casualty ward. Employers look for people who have the following qualities.

- People who take initiatives.
- People who build on their strengths and find ways to contribute to the organisation.
- People who are creative.
- People who can manage change successfully.
- People who are entrepreneurial.

Potential employers need people who will make things happen and take advantage of "empowerment within parameters". On a scale 0—10, how do you rate yourself as being Enterprising?

MY EMPLOYABILITY

Rate yourself on the following characteristics.

Do this on a scale 0—10:

- **Being an encourager**

- **Being enterprising**

- **Being able to achieve excellence**

BEING ABLE TO ACHIEVE EXCELLENCE

"Do you know anybody who is outstanding in our field?" a managing director asked me recently. "If so, put them in touch with me. We can then work out their best contribution to our company." Quality people will always find work, providing they are also willing to make clear contracts about their contribution to achieving the organisation's goals. Potential employers look for people who have the following qualities:

- People who finish things.
- People who find practical solutions to problems.
- People who do superb quality work.
- People who commit themselves to constant improvement.
- People who find new ways to contribute to the organisation.

Employers need people who perform outstanding work. They want such people to build on their strengths, set specific goals and use their talents to benefit the organisation. On a scale 0—10, how do you rate yourself as being able to achieve Excellence?

"I am willing to play my part, but where do I find a good workplace?" you may ask. Try tackling the exercise called My Perfect Employer. Who would be your perfect employer? What benefits can you offer such a sponsor? What basic things must you get right when applying for a job? How can you create a distinctive job application which grabs their attention? What is your action plan for finding your perfect employer? Some people like to work as team-members, but others prefer the challenges of leadership. Let's explore this route to doing work you love.

You can work as a leader

"I am reading a book on leadership, but the message is that you have to be superhuman," said one of my colleagues. "Is there any hope for us mere mortals?" The answer is both "Yes" and "No". First: People must want to be leaders. Second: They must build on their strengths. Third: They must learn how to build successful teams. Providing they are willing to do these things, people can follow the leadership road towards performing creative work.

Good leaders have several things in common. They start by translating

MY PERFECT EMPLOYER

Who would be your perfect employer? What can you offer them? What basic things must you get right when applying for a job? How can you create a distinctive job application to grab their attention? What is your action plan for finding your perfect employer?

My perfect employer would be:

*
....

....

The benefits I would offer this kind of employer would be:

*
....

*
....

*
....

The things I can do to find this kind of employer are:

*
....

*
....

*
....

The basic things I must do right when applying for work with this employer are:

*
....

*
....

*
....

The creative things I can do to grab the employer's attention are:

*
....

*
....

*
....

My action plan for getting work with my perfect employer is:

*
....

*
....

*
....

the team's values into a clear vision. Staff must know what mountain their team is climbing, why they are climbing it and when they will reach the summit. Good leaders inspire people to *want* to climb the mountain. How? They communicate the goals and show the benefits. They also give staff a sense of ownership in implementing their part of the strategy. Encouragement is vital. Good leaders support their staff and ensure they do good quality work. They guide the whole team to success. Staff must be given a chance to celebrate and share in the rewards. It is then time to inspire people to climb the next mountain.

Good leaders often build a leadership team. Why? People are seldom perfect and no one person has all the qualities needed to provide superb leadership in the modern world. "Be who you are, only more so", is the motto. Build on your strengths and find ways to compensate for your weaknesses. Good leaders create a senior team that covers key areas, such as: Vision, People-Management, Implementation, Financial Management, Co-ordination and Achievement. How do you rate your ability in these areas which are vital to running any business? Try tackling the exercise called My Leadership Rating.

VISION

Good leadership teams have people who crystallise the vision. They set goals by starting from their destination, working backwards and clarifying the strategy. Being results-oriented, such people are frequently more concerned with long-term goals, rather than short-term feelings. They demand a lot from their staff. Visionaries also see long-term opportunities within current crises. On a scale 0—10, how do you rate yourself as a visionary?

PEOPLE MANAGEMENT

Good leadership teams encourage people to do their best. Visionaries may be wonderful at leading the column, but people-managers must stay in touch with the troops. They focus on Clarity, Coaching and Creativity. Step One is Clarity. They make sure everybody knows their part in achieving the team's goals. Step Two is Coaching. They give people the encouragement, practical support and help they need to do the job. Step Three is Creativity. They encourage people to take initiatives and use their talents to the benefit of the team. On a scale 0—10, how do you rate yourself as a people-manager?

MY LEADERSHIP RATING

HOW DO YOU RATE YOURSELF AS A LEADER
IN THE FOLLOWING AREAS?

0—10

● VISION

● PEOPLE-MANAGEMENT

● IMPLEMENTATION

● FINANCIAL MANAGEMENT

● CO-ORDINATION

● ACHIEVEMENT

IMPLEMENTATION

Visionaries know what needs to be done; Implementers know how to get things done. Good leadership teams have "Doers" who get the show on the road. They ensure tasks are completed and everybody gets from A to Z. How skilled are you are at making things happen? On a scale 0—10, how do you rate yourself as an implementer? (Simply rate your implementation skills. Whether or not these are the right things to do is immaterial. Many teams score high on implementation, but are doing the wrong things. If they were doing the right things they would be extremely effective.)

FINANCIAL MANAGEMENT

How skilled are you as a financial manager? Leadership teams are responsible for this discipline which covers a wide spectrum. Setting a realistic budget, staying within budget, giving customers value for money, making effective use of money and making a profit.Financial managers have an increasing role to play in teams. They must provide staff with financial support, but also ensure they make good use of money. On a scale 0—10, how do you rate yourself as a financial manager?

CO-ORDINATION

Good leadership teams ensure that all staff continually work together towards achieving their agreed goals. Co-ordination is one of the greatest challenges facing modern teams. Why? People who are encouraged to take initiatives often feel tempted to head off in different directions. Balancing creativity and co-ordination is difficult. It calls for agreeing specific goals, making clear contracts and ensuring people fulfil their agreed contracts. Good teams also co-operate by pooling their talents. They co-ordinate their efforts to make 2 + 2 = 5. On a scale 0—10, how do you rate yourself as a co-ordinator?

ACHIEVEMENT

Leaders are judged by their team's performance. Senior managers face a massive challenge because, while they are answerable for the results, staff are the only people who can deliver success. Vision, people-management, co-ordination and other factors shape the team, but the goal is achievement. Does your team fulfil its purpose? Does it care for its people, products and profits? Does it contribute towards building a better planet? Leaders must be both encouraging and demanding to make sure people produce visible results. On a scale 0—10, how do you rate yourself at ensuring that people achieve the team's goals?

"Are leaders born or made?" is an old question. Everybody is born with some leadership qualities, but individuals choose whether or not to develop these qualities. How do you rate yourself as a leader? You might score high on vision, for example, but low on financial management. Try tackling the following exercise. How can you improve your leadership skills? Take this one step further: imagine you were building a leadership team. How would you build on your personal strengths? How would you compensate for your weaknesses? Leaders must be ready to accept both pleasures and pains, but the same rule applies however you earn money.

"The grass always seems greener on the other side of the hill," said one person on a Career Development workshop. "But now I see that all jobs have an upside and a downside. I must start a job with my eyes open, rather than hope it will fulfil my fantasy." Looking back at the different ways of working, what are the consequences of pursuing each road? Try tackling the exercise called The Three Ways To Work: Recognising the Pluses and Minuses. Describe the rewards and drawbacks involved in working as an individual, as a team member and as a leader. Whichever road you travel, it is important to recognise and accept the whole package.

You can clarify your finishing skills

Before embarking on any road, make sure you have many of the implementation skills needed to complete the journey. "I enjoy writing, so I will become a writer," somebody may say. But writing a book calls for more than putting pen to paper. Writing calls for targeting the book, research, daily discipline, creativity, enjoying the highs, coping with the lows and finding a publisher. It calls for having the stamina to rewrite, rewrite and rewrite. It calls for loving the process, enjoying the journey and reaching the goal. Finishing is a vital skill in the arts, sport, business or any other walk of life.

Everybody has finished things in their lives; everybody has gathered sets of implementation skills. The first step towards doing satisfying work is to clarify what you enjoy doing. The second step is to clarify whether you have the implementation skills needed to pursue your interests successfully. The third step is to clarify how to apply these to skills to future projects. "How do I discover my implementation skills?" you may ask. One way to start is by tackling the exercise called My Finished Projects.

MY LEADERSHIP RATING: HOW I CAN IMPROVE

List the practical steps you can take to improve as a leader in the following areas:

- **VISION**
  - ....
  - ....

- **PEOPLE- MANAGEMENT**
  - ....
  - ....

- **IMPLEMENTATION**
  - ....
  - ....

- **FINANCIAL MANAGEMENT**
  - ....
  - ....

- **CO-ORDINATION**
  - ....
  - ....

- **ACHIEVEMENT**
  - ....
  - ....

THE THREE WAYS TO WORK:

Recognising the pluses and minuses

Describe what you see as the pluses and minuses of each way of working:

Working as an individual

The pluses   The minuses

- ....   - ....

- ....   - ....

- ....   - ....

Working in a team or organisation

- ....   - ....

- ....   - ....

- ....   - ....

Working as a leader

- ....   - ....

- ....   - ....

- ....   - ....

MY FINISHED PROJECTS

Finishing calls for more than having a vision; it calls for developing implementation skills. Applying these skills successfully will ensure that you experience the joy of achieving your vision. This two-part exercise invites you to clarify your implementation skills.

MY PAST PROJECTS

● Describe three projects you have finished successfully in your life.

● Taking each project in turn, write down five or more things you did to manage the process and complete the project successfully.

● Looking back on what you have written about projects you have finished successfully, move on to your future plans.

MY FUTURE PROJECT

● Describe a specific project that you want to complete in the future.

● Describe the specific things you can do to manage the process and complete the project successfully.

● Describe the pluses and minuses involved in completing the project successfully. Providing you are prepared to accept these pluses and minuses, move on to the final part.

● Describe the specific action plans you have for tackling and completing this project.

MY PAST PROJECTS

PROJECT A

● ....

The specific things I did to manage the
process and complete the project successfully:

● ....

● ....

● ....

● ....

● ....

PROJECT B

● ....

The specific things I did to manage the
process and complete the project successfully:

● ....

● ....

● ....

● ....

● ....

PROJECT C

● ....

The specific things I did to manage the
process and complete the project successfully:

● ....

● ....

● ....

● ....

● ....

MY FUTURE PROJECT

The project I want to complete successfully is:

- ....

The specific things I can do to manage the
process and complete the project successfully are:

- ....
- ....
- ....
- ....
- ....

The pluses involved in tackling the project will be:

- ....
- ....
- ....

The minuses involved In tackling the project will be:

- ....
- ....
- ....

My specific action plans for tackling
and completing the project are:

- ....
- ....
- ....
- ....
- ....

You can go around the system to reach your goals

Picture the scene. The time is any afternoon between 1950 and 1980. You are 15 years old, sitting in the secondary school classroom and waiting to hear the Careers Officer give his 30-minute speech. "We are very glad to welcome Mr Smith here today," says the head teacher. "Everybody has been looking forward to his visit and to getting some useful tips about how to be successful in the world of work."

"A prosperous future awaits anybody who is ready to work hard and study," says Mr Smith. "Some people are good with their hands, other people are good with their heads. A boy who is good with his hands can become an apprentice and get a 'trade'. He will have security for life. A girl can become a hairdresser, typist or maybe even a nurse. They will always have something to fall back on later in life. If you are good with your head, I would recommend studying at college or university. People with qualifications will always be able to get a job in our society."

The times were soon changing for Mr Smith and everybody in the classroom. The "old rules" about careers were replaced by "new rules". Sixty per cent of the jobs that will be available in ten years' time, for example, have not yet been invented. How do you prepare yourself for such radical changes? Step One is to develop both your inner qualities and outer qualifications. Step Two is to recognise that "security is to have an alternative" and also to be able to manage change successfully. Step Three is to go around the system to reach your goals. How can you follow these steps in the world of work?

Micke Larsson developed both his inner qualities and outer qualifications. His inner qualities were courage, clarity and creativity. Travelling from village to village, he built High Service into a profitable business. What about outer qualifications? No college offers certificates in Climbing Church Spires, so how could he demonstrate the quality of his work to potential customers? Collecting newspaper articles, photographs and references, Micke followed the path taken by many artists. He created a portfolio of his achievements. Try tackling the following exercise which invites you to catalogue your own successes.

● **My portfolio**

Make a portfolio which shows what you offer to potential employers. This can contain anything which demonstrates what you have created in your work. "But I don't produce anything that people can see," you may say. Use your imagination to make the invisible visible. For example: reports, brochures, quotes from satisfied customers, "before and after" photographs, course materials, books and other examples of your creative work.

"Security comes from getting a good education and finding a steady job," said the old rules. "Security is to have an alternative," say the new rules. What would happen if you lost your job tomorrow? Would you be able to find or invent an even better job? Don't wait for the fateful day. Too many organisations are full of people who cannot see the possibility of finding another job. Make an inventory of your skills and map out an alternative career. Bolstered by this inner strength, you may still choose to remain in your present employment, but the key factor is choice. You are choosing to stay, you don't *have* to stay. Always make sure you have a Plan B.

"People are afraid of change," we are told. But how many changes have you managed in your life: hundreds? thousands? Everybody has a track record of adventuring, exploring and developing. People venture forth to

MY PORTFOLIO

Make a portfolio which shows what you offer to potential employers. This can contain anything which shows what you have created in your work. "But I don't produce anything that people can see," you may say. Use your imagination to make the invisible visible. For example: reports, brochures, quotes from satisfied customers, "before and after" photographs, course materials, books, and other examples of your creative work.

learn skills, change jobs and seek challenges. (There are different kinds of change, of course, such as Reactive Change, Proactive Change and Paradigm Change, which are described in *The Positive Planet.**) People are not afraid of transitions: but they are afraid of being unable to cope with them successfully. They will embrace change when they believe that doing so will: a) be profitable; b) be practical; and c) be virtually guaranteed to produce positive results.

Managing change is a key skill for shaping your future. Try tackling two exercises which focus on your ability to make this happen.

● Managing change successfully

Begin by describing a personal or professional change you have managed successfully in your life. For example: moving to another country, mastering a new skill, getting a fresh job, overcoming a difficult challenge, or whatever. Continue by describing five things you did right to manage the change. Conclude by describing three things you can do to manage changes successfully in the future.

● Changes in the world of work

People can shape the future by anticipating changes. This exercise invites you to write three lists. First: Describe changes in the world of work during the past five years, such as changes in society, organisations, technology,

* By Mike Pegg. Published by Enhance Ltd.

MANAGING CHANGE SUCCESSFULLY

a) Describe a personal or professional change in your life that you have managed successfully.

● When I ....

....

b) What did you do right then? Write five things you did right to manage the change successfully.

● I ....

● I ....

● I ....

● I ....

● I ....

c) Describe three things you can do to manage changes successfully in the future.

● I can ....

● I can ....

● I can ....

CHANGES IN THE WORLD OF WORK

Write three lists. First: What you believe have been the changes in the world of work during the past five years. For example: changes in society, organisations, technology, skills, etc. Second: What you believe may be changes during the next five years. Third: How you can manage these changes successfully.

Changes in the last five years:

- ....
- ....
- ....

Changes in the next five years:

- ....
- ....
- ....

How I can manage these changes successfully:

- I can ....
- I can ....
- I can ....

skills, etc. Second: Describe what you see as possible changes during the next five years, such as shrinking organisations, outsourcing, etc. Third: Describe how you can manage these changes successfully. People who anticipate and stay ahead of such changes are more likely to shape a positive future.

"Pretty soon everybody will have to be an entrepreneur," said Robert Schwartz, founder of the Tarrytown School for Entrepreneurs in New York State. "It is simply the next stage of the human journey to be much more independent." Certainly people will have to grasp the entrepreneur's way of thinking, which involves finding creative ways to reach a goal.

Lasse was 17 when he jumped off engineering school in Sweden. "I enjoy sailing and skiing," he said, "and I want to get a job involved with sailing." Spring was arriving so he looked in the sailing magazines and found seven sail-makers in Stockholm. Lasse wrote to each firm but made his letter distinctive. Describing what he could offer, he enclosed a giant poster of himself making a sail. Five employers offered him interviews and he got a job ahead of 250 applicants. "You must have been crazy to send that poster," said the boss, "but it was the only way you could have got an interview."

People need to recognise there are two ways to reach a goal; the conventional road and the creative road. Lasse could have followed the conventional road by signing on at the local job centre, taking a course, writing a formal letter and waiting for an interview. His chances of success would have been at least 250-1. The creative road meant asking: "What are the real results I want to achieve? How can I do my best to achieve these results? When do I want to try?" Lasse kept his eye on the vision and went around the system to reach his goals.

Sometimes it is best to be conventional; sometimes it is best to be creative. Brain surgeons, pilots and tax officers, for instance, often follow tried and trusted techniques. But the first step is to clarify your real goals. You may want to obtain an MBA, for example, because it once provided a passport to jobs in business. The question remains: "What are the real results you want to achieve?" You may want to find a rewarding job, enjoy a salary or run a company.

At a deeper level, your real aim may be happiness. At the present time you see the MBA as a necessary qualification along the road. But there may be better ways to achieve what you want out of life. Establish the real "What?" and the "How?" will fall into place. You will find many other creative ways to reach your goals. Let's focus on your vision for doing work you love.

THE CREATIVE ROAD TOWARDS REACHING YOUR GOALS

There are different ways to reach your goals. One way is to follow the conventional route through the system. Another way is to take the creative road and go around the system to reach your goals.

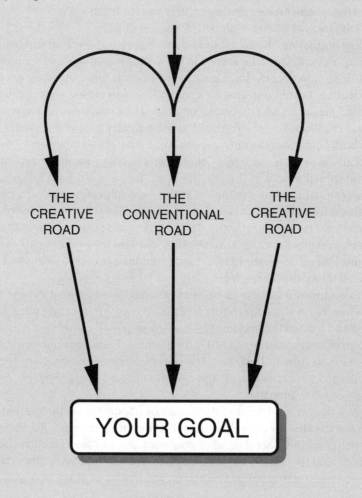

THE CREATIVE ROAD   THE CONVENTIONAL ROAD   THE CREATIVE ROAD

YOUR GOAL

Step Two:
VISION

"I WOULD like to follow my vision, but it hasn't appeared yet," somebody may say. "Doesn't it come to you in a blinding flash?"

Sometimes it does, but often after years of hard work. Anita Roddick is believed to have started with a vision about shaping the Body Shop into a global company. She disagrees. Building on an ethical business idea, her first aim was to get enough customers to feed her family, repay the bank and pay the rent of her shop in Brighton. Anita saw the potential of the Body Shop after both successes and setbacks. She then pursued her picture with single-minded devotion. Visions appear after years of practice.

The Lion Man is devoted to translating his vision into a reality. "I want to tell you a story about lions," he declares, prowling the theatre stage. The 200-strong business audience sits transfixed. Springing from behind a bush, he shouts: "This is how the female lion attacks. She can break the jaw of an antelope with one smash of her claws." He leaps from the stage and extends his crooked hand towards the front row. Taking an intake of breath, the audience shrink back in their seats. Who is The Lion Man?

Ian Thomas spent eight years living wild in the South African bush. Since publishing his book *The Power of The Pride*, he travels the globe teaching how lions work in teams. "I am only talking about lions," he says, "but they provide many lessons about teamwork." Fascinating and a bit frightening, Ian earns up to £2,000 for his two-hour performance. The money is ploughed back into his first love, returning to the wild to study his favourite lion pack. The Lion Man follows a path taken by many explorers throughout history. He packages and sells his know-how to interested people, who provide the financial backing for him to pursue his real goal in life.

Christina Noble is a former street child who now helps other street children. Growing up in Dublin's slums, she was disowned by her alcoholic father shortly after her mother died. She spent much of her childhood in a loveless orphanage. Returning to Dublin as a teenager, Christina spent her days on the streets and her nights sleeping in a graveyard. One night she was pulled into a car by four men and repeatedly raped.

Christina sought a new life by travelling to England. Settling in Birmingham, she married a violent husband, suffered several miscarriages and gave birth to three children. Attempting to leave her husband, she was committed to mental hospital and diagnosed as schizophrenic. Doctors subjected her to massive doses of electro-convulsive therapy.

Writing in *Bridge Across My Sorrows*, Christina describes how she broke free from the past to run a catering business. Since the early 1970s she nurtured an old dream, however, believing her future lay on the other side of the world.

"In early 1989 I sensed that my life was coming into another period," she writes. "I thought of little but Vietnam. In my mind's eye I could see a little girl in the dream reaching out to me." Christina met a man who took up a job in Ho Chi Minh City. One day he rang to say: "If you really want to work with children, there is plenty of opportunity here. The streets are overrun with destitute children. They are everywhere. And they need your help."

Christina found her calling at the age of 45. She caught a plane, arrived in Ho Chi Minh City and rented a small room at the Rex Hotel. She began work immediately. Meeting two orphaned girls on the street, she smuggled them into the hotel. She fed them, bathed them and dressed them in fresh clothes. After knocking on the guests' doors to collect money, Christina caused chaos by throwing a Christmas Day party for 200 street children in the restaurant at the Rex Hotel. She threw herself into a whirlwind of activities. By 1991, two years after arriving, she had swept past bureaucrats to open a well-equipped Medical and Social Centre and create an International Foundation with almost £100,000 in a London bank. Every penny has been used to serve the children.

Reporters compare Christina with Mother Teresa, but she sees little resemblance, arguing: "I am no saint, I am wild." She sings, swears, drinks double whiskies and harangues conferences about children's rights. Pouncing like an angry lioness, she physically attacks tourists who try to abuse street children. Christina writes: "When I began here in Vietnam, people said what I wanted to do was impossible. 'You are only one person,' they said. But when I was a child, I needed only one person to understand my suffering and pain, one person to love me. One is very important. There are many ones, and they add up." Mama Tina, as she is known, continues to give love to the street children of Ho Chi Minh City.

People who do work they love translate their values into a clear vision. How can you make this happen? One way to begin is by taking the next step.

You can clarify your possibilities

Kevin held down a telephone sales job in a training company. Returning from work after the Christmas holidays, however, he discovered the spring had gone from his step. "I find it hard to get excited about selling," he said, "and that is deadly in my job."

Kevin clarified his alternatives by tackling the exercise called My Future Life. He drew a map of the possible roads he could travel in the next six months, 18 months and three years. He also described the possible pluses and minuses of travelling each road.

Kevin's first road was the predictable. Staying at the training company, he could sweat to exceed his sales targets and boost his salary. Promotion would give him and Juanita, his Spanish wife, the financial security to buy a bigger house. Kevin's second road involved a radical change in direction. During the past three years he had spent many nights as a volunteer counsellor at a drop-in centre. Rewarding as it was listening to people, he preferred something more businesslike.

Researching the options, he found that the local university offered a qualification in career counselling. Pursuing this option meant less money but more satisfaction. Kevin's third road involved working at his in-laws' holiday complex in Spain, building the golfing side of the business and becoming a partner in the company. After completing his drawing, he listed the pluses and minuses of travelling each road.

Kevin considered the different options and the consequences. Looking at the map, he then drew the road he really wanted to travel. How? He circled the best parts of each route and joined these parts together to create a new road. After discussing the options with Juanita, Kevin chose to become a career counsellor.

The course began in September, so the next few months meant saving money. During the year-long programme he could earn cash by doing evening telephone sales. The course focused on helping young people, but Kevin's real desire was to work with adults. He aimed to spend two years in the career service, then join an out-placement agency and earn a good salary.

Juanita liked her work in a local hotel but, within the next few years, she wanted to find a house in the country and start a family. Five years down the line Kevin planned to start his own business helping adults to change their careers. Spain did not figure in either his or Juanita's plans, but it remained a fall-back option. Holidaying golfers might want help to create a more positive future.

Try tackling the exercise called My Future Life. First: Draw a map of the possible roads you can follow in the next six months, 18 months and three years. Add the possible pluses and minuses of each road. You may then wish to discuss your map with a friend to explain each of the roads. Second: Draw the road you really want to travel. Begin by circling the best parts of each route. Be creative and use your imagination to draw a road which includes all these parts. (Bear in mind that you can tackle several of your chosen activities in parallel; you need not wait for years to do what you love.) Plan how you can follow this chosen road and build in some early successes.

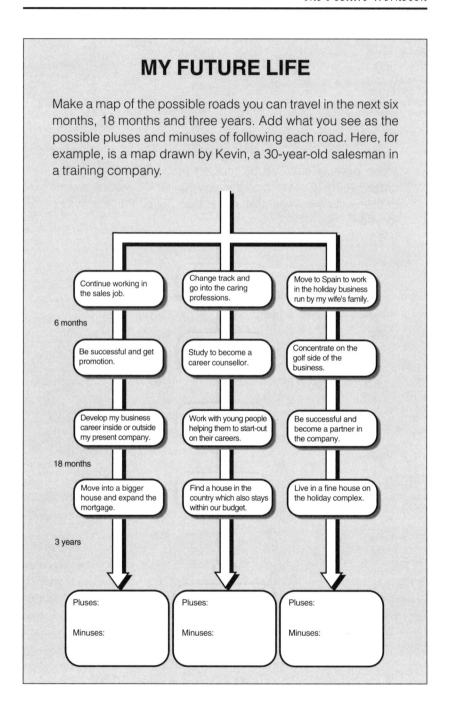

MY FUTURE LIFE

Make a map of the possible roads you can travel in the next six months, 18 months and three years. Add what you see as the possible pluses and minuses of following each road. Here, for example, is a map drawn by Kevin, a 30-year-old salesman in a training company.

Continue working in the sales job.

Change track and go into the caring professions.

Move to Spain to work in the holiday business run by my wife's family.

6 months

Be successful and get promotion.

Study to become a career counsellor.

Concentrate on the golf side of the business.

Develop my business career inside or outside my present company.

Work with young people helping them to start-out on their careers.

Be successful and become a partner in the company.

18 months

Move into a bigger house and expand the mortgage.

Find a house in the country which also stays within our budget.

Live in a fine house on the holiday complex.

3 years

Pluses:

Minuses:

Pluses:

Minuses:

Pluses:

Minuses:

MY FUTURE LIFE

Complete the exercise by drawing the road you really want to follow. How? Begin by drawing circles round what you see as the best parts of each road. Follow this by being creative and using your imagination to draw a road which includes all of these parts. Conclude by making plans for following this chosen road. (Bear in mind that you can tackle several of your chosen activities in parallel, rather than put off these activities for years).

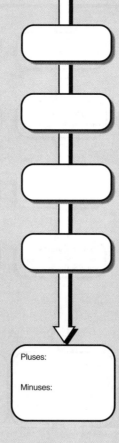

6 months

18 months

3 years

Pluses:

Minuses:

Christina Noble, Ian Thomas and Anita Roddick followed a route taken by many people who do creative work. They explored a number of alternatives before committing themselves to achieving a specific vision. The next few pages provide exercises you can use to consider your options.

● Ten things I want to do in my life

Describe ten things you want to do in your life. One person began their list by writing: "I Want: To help my son find work he enjoys; To travel to Australia and New Zealand; To run my own small company, etc."

● My ideal life

Draw or describe your ideal life. Where would you be living? Who would be living with you? How would you spend your days? What would be your work? What would you be creating to give to other people? After outlining your ideal life, clarify the concrete steps you can take to make this happen.

● £1 million

What would you do if you won £1 million? Begin the exercise by describing what you would do if you had this amount of cash. Money can help you to get some of these things quicker, but it cannot guarantee you happiness. Satisfaction often comes from learning to enjoy the journey as well as enjoying the result. Conclude the exercise by using your imagination to find specific steps you can take towards achieving some of these goals in your present life.

● My money

Many people in the richer countries can live on far less than they spend. How much do you really need to live? Calculate the actual amount you need to bring in from your work. People who tackle this exercise often discover they are spending money on things they do not need. Providing they budget correctly, they can live on less money and gain the freedom to do work they enjoy.

● A letter from your employer

The letter from your employer on a later page says that, due to redundancies, you are being given three months' notice, plus an extra three months' wages.

The exercise challenges you to spend an hour creating your new job. The only stipulation is that you cannot apply for a full-time job with one employer. (This is a good exercise to give to people on workshops. Each person can then present their new job to other people in the group.)

● My white room

Imagine that your life is an empty white room with nothing in it except your family. Starting afresh, you can put who and what you want in your white room. Describe or draw the three people, three talents, three goals, three possessions and three other things you would put in your white room.

● Two years to live

What would you do if you only had two years to live? Clarify your priorities during this time. Can you do anything towards pursuing these aims in the next few months? Write the specific things you can do to concentrate on your priorities in life. Taking steps towards doing these things will ensure that you are focusing on your A1 goals.

● My obituary

Take half an hour to sit down by yourself and write your own obituary. You can write or create this in any way you wish. After completing your work, you may wish to share it with another person. Finally, consider how you can devote more of your time to the important things that emerged for you when writing your obituary. (Some people may find this exercise difficult, so be careful if you introduce it on a course. Emphasise that people should only tackle it if they believe it will be valuable. The exercise is often used in American secondary schools, however, to help teenagers define their life goals. It also forms part of the Harvard Business School programme on Career Development.)

● My offerings to my customers

Describe what you offer to your customers. You may provide them with tangible products, such as delicious meals, attractive paintings, specific skills or whatever. You may also provide more intangible things, such as a good experience, excellent service or instant recovery from any mistakes. Later we will explore how to integrate what you want to offer with what your customers want.

● **My best contribution to my organisation**

Perhaps you prefer to stay in your present organisation, rather than become a freelance worker. How can you use your talents to help it to reach its goals? First: Describe what you believe to be your best contribution to your organisation. Second: Describe the pluses and minuses of taking this role — for yourself, for the organisation and for the customers. Third: Describe the specific steps you can take towards making this contribution. You may need to make clear contracts with your sponsors, for example, set specific goals and deliver early successes. This is a good exercise to give to all people who want to make a creative contribution to achieving their organisation's goals.

TEN THINGS I WANT
TO DO IN MY LIFE

I want:

● To ....

● To ....

● To ....

● To ....

● To ....

● To ....

● To ....

● To ....

● To ....

● To ....

MY IDEAL LIFE

What would be your ideal life? Use this page to draw and describe your ideal life. Then focus on concrete steps you can take to make this happen.

My ideal life would be:

£1 MILLION

What would you do if you won £1 million? Begin the exercise by describing what you would do if you had this amount. Money can help you to get some of these things quicker, but it cannot guarantee you happiness. Satisfaction often comes from learning to enjoy the journey as well as enjoying the result. Conclude the exercise by using your imagination to find specific steps you can take towards achieving some of these goals in your present life.

If I had £1 million I would:

- ....
- ....
- ....
- ....
- ....

**How I can take steps towards
doing some of these things in my life:**

- ....
- ....
- ....

MY MONEY

Many people in the richer countries can live on far less than they spend. How much do you really need to live? Calculate the actual amount you need to bring in from your work. Many people who tackle this exercise discover they are spending money on things they do not need. Providing they budget correctly, they can live on less money and gain the freedom to do work they enjoy. Make a list of the money you need to live and work.

ITEM   **£**

- ....   - ....
- ....   - ....
- ....   - ....
- ....   - ....
- ....   - ....
- ....   - ....
- ....   - ....
- ....   - ....
- ....   - ....

Total: £ ....

A LETTER FROM YOUR EMPLOYER

Read the following letter from your employer and then tackle the exercise.

Dated Yesterday

Dear........................,

We regret to announce that, due to financial circumstances, we are being forced to make redundancies. Unfortunately you are one of the people for whom there will not be a job in the future. Consequently we are offering you three months' notice plus a further payment for three months.

We thank you for all your efforts and wish you good luck in pursuing your future career.

Yours faithfully,

....
Managing Director

Take one hour to create your future job and make a poster headed My Future Work. There is one condition: you cannot apply for a full-time job in an organisation. Present your poster to a group of people and also describe your plans for getting this kind of job.

MY WHITE ROOM

The White Room exercise invites you to focus on the people, goals and other things that are really important to you in life. Imagine that your life is an empty white room with nothing in it except your family. You are beginning afresh and have the chance to put what you want in your white room. Write or draw the three people, three talents, three goals, three possessions and three other things you would put in your white room.

The three people:

- ....
- ....
- ....

The three talents:

- ....
- ....
- ....

The three goals:

- ....
- ....
- ....

The three possessions:

- ....
- ....
- ....

The three other things:

- ....
- ....
- ....

You may wish to consider devoting more time and energy to focusing on these things in the future.

TWO YEARS TO LIVE

What would you do if you only had two years to live? Write down all the things that you would do.

I would:

- ....
- ....
- ....
- ....
- ....

Can you do anything towards doing some of these things now and in the next few months? Write the things you want to do.

I want:

- ....
- ....
- ....
- ....

Taking steps towards doing these things will help to ensure that you are focusing on your A1 goals in life.

MY OBITUARY

Take half an hour to sit down by yourself and write your own obituary. You can write or create this in any way you wish. After completing your work, you may wish to share it with another person. Finally: Consider how you can devote more of your time to the important things that emerged for you when writing your obituary.

MY OFFERINGS
TO MY CUSTOMERS

Describe the things that you want to offer to your customers. These can be tangible things, such as specific products, and the more intangible things, such as the experience of good service.

**The things I want to
offer to my customers are:**

● ....

....

....

● ....

....

....

● ....

....

....

MY BEST CONTRIBUTION
TO MY ORGANISATION

**I believe my best contribution
to my organisation would be:**

- ....
- ....
- ....

The pluses for the organisation would be:

- ....
- ....
- ....

The minuses for the organisation would be:

- ....
- ....
- ....

The steps I can take towards making this contribution are:

- ....
- ....
- ....

You can clarify what your customers want

Ian Thomas, the Lion Man, translates his passion into a profession. Studying wildlife remains his obsession, but how can he get financial backing? People who make a living doing what they love ask questions like: "What are my strengths? Who are my potential customers? How can I integrate what I want to offer with what my customers want? How can I give them superb service?" Ian builds on his strengths - safari trips, public speaking and writing - and then follows a well-trodden trail. The Lion Man offers the right product to the right people at the right price in the right way to get the right results.

"There is always a market for quality work," we are told, but this statement hides several challenges. The first challenge is to offer quality products. Ian Thomas offers safari trips, speeches and his book *The Power of The Pride*. Books increase credibility, but seldom bring in a living wage. His unique talent is giving inspiring presentations showing how lions achieve peak performance.

The second challenge is to identify the right niche, which is difficult in a world of expanding choice. Ian targets people in business. Why? They have the money, want good conference speakers and can apply the ideas in their work. The third challenge is reaching and selling to people in this niche. Ian

DOING WORK YOU LOVE

It is vital to offer:
- The right product
  to
- The right people
  at
- The right price
  in
- The right way
  to get
- The right results

gets work via safari contacts, the book and recommendations from satisfied customers.

"My aim is to build a better world," somebody may say, "I find difficulty using this type of business language." Charity workers often follow similar principles, but they talk in terms of focusing their efforts to tackle specific problems. Christina Noble builds on her strengths, for example, to assist street children in Ho Chi Minh City. She has made her personal commitment and, in her own mind, is offering the right thing to the right people in the right way.

Caring people can find the commitment process to be painful. Why? Choosing to help some people means excluding others who may be suffering. The only consolation is that other charity workers may provide for other groups in need. Discussing money may also be distasteful. But who will pick up the bill? Christina recognises that street children can only offer thanks, but she must get funding. Employing her business skills, she travels the world to get sponsors. The Foundation needs more than good will. It needs cash, medicines and equipment to help the children in Vietnam.

How do you turn your passion into a profession? Get somebody to pay you for doing it. Building on your strengths, start by clarifying what you want to offer people. The next steps are: a) To identify all your potential "customers". b) To identify what your customers want. The following pages provide exercises you can use to tackle these challenges. (Some people prefer the terms "stakeholders" or "clients", rather than "customers". Use the word that you prefer.) The next step will be to explore both how to maintain your integrity and satisfy these people who pay your wages.

● My potential customers

Draw a map which shows all your potential customers. (If you work within an organisation, this should include both internal and external customers.) After completing the map, describe three things you believe each of these customers wants. Display this map in a place where you can see it every day.

● My perfect customer

Who would be your perfect customer: individuals, teams or organisations? What would you offer them? What would they want to buy? Why would they buy your product or service? What would they see as the benefits? What would they be prepared to pay? Where would they be located? How often would they buy your service or product? Describe your perfect customer.

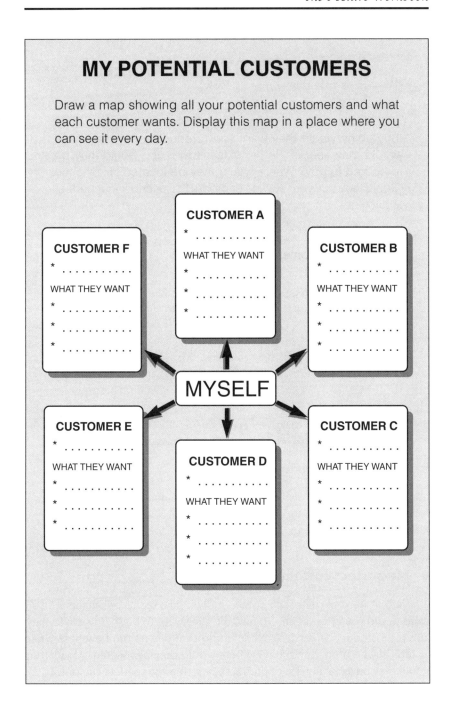

MY POTENTIAL CUSTOMERS

Draw a map showing all your potential customers and what each customer wants. Display this map in a place where you can see it every day.

CUSTOMER A
* . . . .
WHAT THEY WANT
* . . . .
* . . . .
* . . . .

CUSTOMER F
* . . . .
WHAT THEY WANT
* . . . .
* . . . .
* . . . .

CUSTOMER B
* . . . .
WHAT THEY WANT
* . . . .
* . . . .
* . . . .

MYSELF

CUSTOMER E
* . . . .
WHAT THEY WANT
* . . . .
* . . . .
* . . . .

CUSTOMER D
* . . . .
WHAT THEY WANT
* . . . .
* . . . .
* . . . .

CUSTOMER C
* . . . .
WHAT THEY WANT
* . . . .
* . . . .
* . . . .

MY PERFECT CUSTOMER

Who would be your perfect customer? Would they be individuals, teams or organisations? What would they want to buy? Why would they want your product or service? What would they see as the benefits? How much would they be prepared to pay? Where would they be located? How often would they buy your service or product? Describe your perfect customer.

My perfect customer would be:

- ....
....
....

- ....
....
....

- ....
....
....

You can integrate what you want to offer with what your customers want

Eric Maisel describes an age-old dilemma in his book *Staying Sane in the Arts*. The artist may say: "I want to paint potatoes, but the public want peaches. If I paint potatoes, I will go bankrupt. If I paint peaches, I will lose my integrity." Each person must make his or her own decision when tackling this challenge. Some people go bankrupt, some find sponsors for painting potatoes, some go commercial. Some paint sweet potatoes. How can you stay true to yourself and satisfy your customers?

Archie Duncanson, author of *Ecology Begins At Home*, has managed this challenge by maintaining a healthy balance between his mission and mortgage. Choosing to live on £10,000 per year, he practises what he preaches. He is smart at gathering income, however, and aims to reach a certain target group. His lectures and book are aimed at people who are willing to pay to find practical ways to care for their homes and their planet.

Sharing his know-how, he matches their interests and also opens their eyes to new possibilities. He follows a tried and tested formula. Archie does what he believes in, targets a specific type of customer and provides a rewarding experience. This is also a good way to attract future business. Balancing your mission and mortgage calls for being able:

- To build on your strengths and clarify what you want to offer to potential customers.
- To spend a great deal of time and effort doing research to find, target and reach the right customer niche.
- To understand the customers' agenda; to know what they want in their life and work.
- To integrate what you want to offer with what the customers want, and to offer them something of real take-home value.
- To do superb quality work which offers specific benefits to the customers.

Finding the right product to offer to the right people in the right way can take years. One way to start is by creating a customer brochure. Why? It forces you to clarify what you offer to the market. People often write two versions before completing their final brochure.

The first brochure is written for themselves. While this is a vital step, like writing an autobiography before penning other books, the main purpose is to clarify their own philosophy. People sometimes make the mistake of mailing out this brochure. The second brochure is aimed at the market. It is written in a style that speaks directly to customers. Brochures are produced in different styles, shapes and sizes. Broadly speaking, however, they fall into three categories:

● The "Buy Me" brochure

This brochure starts with an autobiographical piece. It reads something like: "I am x years old and have been through pains and pleasures in my life. Because of my experience, you should buy me." The corporate version reads something like: "We are the best company in the world and therefore you should buy us." Otherwise known as the "We Are Wonderful" brochure, it is self-absorbed. It seldom mentions how the customer will benefit.

● The "Success Stories" brochure

This brochure starts with a list of success stories. It reads something like: "Company A came to us with a problem. They wanted the following things to happen: a)........ b)......... c)......... I/We provided the following solution. Company A were delighted. Company B came to us with a problem. They wanted......etc." This type of brochure can be effective, providing it shows potential clients that there is scope for customised solutions.

● The "Customer Benefits" brochure

This brochure is customer focused. Starting with the customer's agenda, it demonstrates you understand their issues, it offers possible solutions and it shows customer benefits. There are many ways to write this kind of brochure. Put in parody form, however, it may read something like: "Would you like to be even happier? . . . Would you like your staff to be even more creative? . . . Would you like to build an even more successful company? If so, read on . . . We can help you to reach these goals." Grabbing the reader is vital. They must see how hiring this person or company will be to their benefit.

My Brochure is an exercise which invites you to clarify what you offer customers. One design factor is worth bearing in mind. Successful brochures sometimes combine all three of the approaches mentioned, but they place them in reverse order.

First: They highlight the customer benefits. Second: They highlight their own success stories in helping customers. Third: They highlight their own expertise. Good brochures show an awareness of the customer's agenda. They are user-friendly, easy to read and inspire people to want to buy. Providing you have clarified what you plan to offer customers, the next step is to finalise your vision.

MY BROCHURE

Create a brochure which shows what you can offer customers. Many people need to write two different kinds of brochure on the way to completing their final brochure. The first brochure is for themselves and helps to clarify their philosophy. While this is a vital step, it may not speak directly to the customers. The second brochure is aimed at the market and outlines the benefits to the customers. Create a brochure which you could give to potential customers.

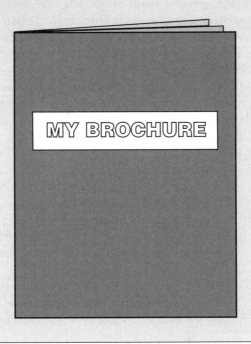

You can clarify your vision

"I prefer the words mission and goals, rather than vision," somebody may say. "Does it matter?" No. Use the words that motivate you to make things happen. Peak Performers talk about visions because they often think in pictures. They have a clear picture of something they want to create, achieve or finish. Starting with a clear image in their heads, they then work backwards. They devote their lives to translating the picture into reality. (Charles Garfield describes this process in his book *Peak Performers*.) People are different, however, so use whatever word inspires you to clarify and climb your particular mountain.

Matt Busby had a vision. Looking across Manchester United's bomb-damaged ground after the war, he vowed to build a club based on "success with style". Twenty-five years later he looked back on creating a series of majestic teams and nurturing thrilling players such as Duncan Edwards, Tommy Taylor, Bobby Charlton, Dennis Law and George Best.

His teams both captured the public imagination and lifted trophies. They won the FA Cup twice, the League Championship four times and the European Cup. The greatest team of all, his 1958 Busby Babes, was destroyed on a snow-covered airfield in Munich. Matt often demonstrated the ability to rebuild from catastrophe. Inheriting a derelict Old Trafford in 1946, he had a clear picture in his head. David Miller, author of *Father of Football*, describes Matt's vision:

"I wanted a different kind of football club from what was normal at the time. There wasn't the human approach. I wanted to manage a team the way I thought the players wanted it . . . I did not set out to build a team: the task ahead was much bigger than that. What I really embarked upon was the building of a system which would produce not one team but four or five, each occupying a rung on the ladder, the summit of which was the first XI."

Matt Busby was a leader in almost every football development, writes David Miller. Manchester United pioneered the creation of a national scouting network to recruit promising young players, many of whom formed the nucleus of the Busby Babes. Despite the threat of sanctions from the Football Association, they became the first English team to enter the European Cup. Old Trafford took a pride in providing United's fans with the best club stadium in the country. Matt Busby produced magical teams and footballers, but he did not believe that success should be bought at any price. On being made a Freeman of the City of Manchester in November 1967, he said:

"I won't deny that it is pleasant to succeed in what you strive to do, but winning matches at all costs is not the test of true achievement. There is nothing wrong in trying to win, so long as you don't set the prize above the game. There is no dishonour in defeat, so long as you play to the limit of your strength and skill. What matters above all is that the game should be played in the right spirit, with the utmost resource of skill and courage, with fair play and no favour, with every man playing as a member of a team, the result accepted without bitterness or conceit."

People often use the three keywords for being creative when clarifying their vision. They ask themselves: "What? How? When?" (See next exercise). Step One is to ask: "What are the real results I want to achieve?" It is vital to clarify the real "What?" before rushing to the "How?". Step Two is to ask: "How can I do my best to achieve this result?" Providing the "What?" is right, the "How?" is often relatively simple. Step Three is to ask: "When do I want to achieve this result?". People need to spend a considerable time on the "What?" when clarifying their vision, otherwise they start climbing the wrong mountain.

What are the real results you want to achieve? The Contented Fisherman had a clear "What?" He wanted to care for the earth, enjoy life and be happy. Not for him the industrial dream of building a large fleet, selling the company and living off the profits. Matt Busby's "What?" was to look beyond creating a winning team. He wanted to build a football club that groomed superb players, won trophies and achieved "success with style". He also wanted Manchester United to become admired around the world.

You may say, for example, "I want to write a book". But what are your real goals: to write a book, publish a book or communicate ideas that will change the world? Buddhists invite each of us to ask ourselves the question: "What do I truly need to be happy?" So what are the real results you want to achieve?

Barbara Winter, author of *Making a Living Without a Job*, also believes in spending a lot of time on the "What?". Pursuing a new direction calls for creating a new vision. People short-circuit success by prematurely imposing a three-letter word on their dreams, she says. That word is "How?", the most powerful dream-basher invented. The solution? Whenever you hear the "How?" question, respond by refocusing on the "What?" Barbara maintains this is the method employed by most successful goal-achievers.

She writes: "Thomas Watson and Joyce Hall knew what they wanted to do: help people communicate better. They accomplished that by not giving too much thought at first to how they were going to do it. Better

The three keywords for being creative: What? How? When?

You can ask yourself:

1) What is the real result I want to achieve?

- Focus on one goal at a time. Make the goal super-specific.

- Clarify the real results you want to achieve by reaching the goal.

- Clarify the pluses and minuses involved in reaching the goal. Complete the "What?" before moving on to the "How?"

2) How can I do my best to achieve this result?

- Say: "I can . . . " and brainstorm lots of ideas.

- First: Go for quantity of ideas. Second: Go for quality of ideas.

- Choose the strategies most likely to succeed.

3) When do I want to achieve this result?

- Make a specific action plan for achieving the goal.

- Re-confirm that you are prepared to accept both the pluses and minuses involved in achieving the goal.

- Start work, encourage yourself and get some early successes.

communication was their obsession. Eventually, each of them found a way to do that. Watson founded IBM; Hall started the company we now know as Hallmark Cards. If you can keep bringing your attention back to what it is you want to do (for example, I want to live in a log house in Vermont and be joyfully jobless), finding out how you can accomplish that becomes easier.

"A woman in Connecticut left my class determined to do something she'd dreamed of since the sixth grade — travel to Nepal. As she kept her attention on what she wanted, she realised that she had just what she needed to achieve this dream. She quit her job with an insurance company and put her energy into making jewellery, a long-time hobby. Not only did this give her a new income source; she had a portable business which funded her travels as she went. A subscriber once sent me a sign that read, 'Obstacles are what you see when you take your eyes off the goal.' Your dreams do not need to be defended by plans about how they will be accomplished, especially not at first. You do, however, have to protect them by focusing on what those dreams are."

What is your vision? The following pages provide exercises you can use to clarify your "What?". Starting with a general exercise, they move into being more specific. Adapt the words and exercises to fit your preferred method for goal-setting.

● My life theme

Look back at the earlier exercises, such as Thirty Things I Enjoy Doing, My Passions, When Do I Feel Most Creative? and My Finished Projects. Can you find any common theme running through what you have written? "My main theme is 'Nurturing People'", said one woman on a Career Development workshop. So we explored how to make a living expressing this theme. Can you find any themes in what you find rewarding in life?

● My priorities

"There are so many things I want to do," you may say, "the hard part is to decide on the most important." This exercise invites you to focus on your priorities. Begin by writing a list of the "projects" you would like to tackle. Getting a certain job, spending time with your grandchildren, writing a book, etc. Looking at your list, rate how important it is for you to do these individual projects. Rate each of them on a scale 0—10. You may then decide to commit yourself only to tackling those projects which rate as at least a 9 out of 10.

● **My headstone**

What would you like written on your headstone? Although a difficult exercise, many people find it helps to sum up their main goal in life. One woman wrote: "She helped young people to develop their gifts." One man wrote: "He created three beautiful books which gave people hope." Nobody has yet written: "He always stayed late at the office." Somebody I know keeps a picture of their headstone in their study. It has become a guiding vision for their daily life. They ask themselves each morning: "What am I going to do today that will contribute to what I want to have written on my headstone?"

● **My purpose on the planet**

Similar to the My Headstone exercise, this focuses on your reason for living. What are your talents? What do you want to create? How can you encourage other people? How can you make the world a better place? What are you here to do, finish or leave behind? Describe what you see as your purpose on the planet.

● **My vision**

People find this challenging exercise helps to clarify their vision. Begin by creating a one-sentence goal which sums up your vision. Then take the following steps. First: Describe your three main goals in your work. Add any sub-goals which form part of your main goals. Second: Describe the pluses and minuses involved in reaching your goals. For yourself, your customers and any other groups. Third: Describe the support you need to reach your goals. Fourth: Describe the measures that will show you have reached your goals. Keep things simple and specific.

One teacher wrote his first main goal as: "I want to encourage the students in my class." A commendable life-principle, but how to recognise when he had reached the target? After some discussion he wrote: "I want to make sure that all 30 of my students can describe three things they do well." It sounds deceptively simple, but it is measurable. The teacher added a time frame. He wanted to achieve this target by the end of the school year. Let's explore how to translate your words into positive action and achieve your vision.

MY LIFE THEME

Look back at the earlier exercises, such as Thirty Things I Enjoy Doing, My Passions, When Do I Feel Most Creative? and My Finished Projects. Can you find any common theme running through what you have written? "My main theme is 'Nurturing People'," said one woman on a Career Development workshop. So we explored how to make a living expressing this theme. Can you find any themes in what you find rewarding in life?

My life themes are:

● ....

....

....

● ....

....

....

● ....

....

....

MY PRIORITIES

This exercise invites you to focus on your priorities. Begin by writing a list of the "projects" you would like to tackle. Getting a certain job, spending time with your grandchildren, writing a book, etc. Looking at your list, rate how important it is for you to do these individual projects. Rate each of them on a scale 0—10. You may then decide to tackle those projects which have the highest rating.

I want to do the following things:

1) ....

The importance to me of doing this is: . . . ./10

2) ....

The importance to me of doing this is: . . . ./10

3) ....

The importance to me of doing this is: . . . ./10

4) ....

The importance to me of doing this is: . . . ./10

5) ....

The importance to me of doing this is: . . . ./10

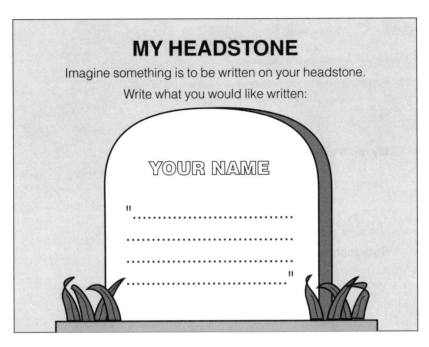

MY HEADSTONE

Imagine something is to be written on your headstone.
Write what you would like written:

YOUR NAME

" ....
....
....
.... "

MY PURPOSE ON THE PLANET

Describe what you see as your purpose on the planet:

**MY PURPOSE
ON THE PLANET IS:**

....
....
....
....

MY VISION

Create a one-sentence goal which sums up your vision

● ....

My main goals are:

I want:

1) To ....

Sub-goals:

    ● To ....

    ● To ....

    ● To ....

2) To ....

    ● To ....

    ● To ....

    ● To ....

3) To ....

    ● To ....

    ● To ....

    ● To ....

THE PLUSES AND MINUSES

Describe the pluses and minuses involved in achieving your goals:

| PLUSES | MINUSES |

FOR MYSELF

- ....
- ....
- ....

- ....
- ....
- ....

FOR THE CUSTOMERS

- ....
- ....
- ....

- ....
- ....
- ....

FOR ANY OTHER GROUPS

- ....
- ....
- ....

- ....
- ....
- ....

THE SUPPORT

The support I would like in order to be able to reach the goals is:

1) ....

....

2) ....

....

3) ....

....

Write down all the practical, financial and emotional support you would like in order to help you to achieve the vision.

THE MEASURES

I will know I have reached the goals when the following happen:

1) ....

....

2) ....

....

3) ....

....

Describe what will be happening that will tell you that you have achieved your vision. Describe this as concretely as possible.

You can clarify your strategy

Vision is knowing "What?" you want to do. Strategy is knowing "How?" to do it. People who achieve their vision follow many of the guidelines we have already mentioned. They build on their strengths, study good models and find out what works. Stressing customer benefits, they offer the right product to the right target group in the right way. They get the right balance between creativity, customers and cash. They work hard, reach their goals and focus on constant improvement. Let's look at somebody who is building a business in what he first found to be disconcerting territory.

Steve always enjoyed solving physical problems. Lego bricks and Meccano kits were his favourite toys in childhood. Repairing bikes and cars occupied his teenage years. Nobody was surprised when he chose an engineering career in a multi-national company.

Steve's life changed shortly after his thirtieth birthday. Playing football for the company team, he was hit by a crunching tackle which damaged his knee. Treatment repaired the ligaments, but his football days were over. Steve's fight to heal his knee triggered an interest in massage and physiotherapy. Previously a rather "conservative" person, he enrolled on a reputable course in complementary medicine. One year later he gained his first massage qualification. Some of his old friends asked: "Has he gone crazy?"

Steve's engineering job continued to provide a steady income, but he wanted to pursue his new interest, preferably earning money using massage skills. "There is a natural health centre in the town," he said, "but I feel uncomfortable with the incense and astrology. Besides, the centre already has five people who offer massage, so I won't get enough clients to build a full-time business."

Steve began to look around for good models. What would be the most suitable profession? What would be the right market niche? He must find clients willing to pay the type of fees that would fund his next qualification and future business.

He chose to specialise in sports massage. Steve's target group was football clubs, rugby clubs, company sports clubs, health centres and gymnasiums. Starting on a voluntary basis, he gave a demonstration to a local rugby team. Steve arrived dressed in a formal suit, changed into a white uniform and showed the players different types of massage. The club invited him back to give massage before their matches. Three months later he got his first pay cheque after meeting the club's request to assist in the recovery of two injured players.

Steve got the club's permission to include this "success story", complete with picture, in his first brochure. Six months later he had three other paying clients: a gymnasium, a football club and the sports centre at his own engineering company. He now earns £30 an hour, practises ten hours a week and uses the money to fund his first qualification in physiotherapy. Steve now aims to make a "Serious Plan" about running a full-time business.

Building a business calls for getting the right balance between Creativity, Customers and Cash. Anita Roddick pursued a creative idea when starting the Body Shop. No doubt she carried scores of imaginative projects in her head, but the first priority was to feed her family. She applied her tradeskills to get customers. They provided the cash to implement other ideas for building the Body Shop.

Thrilled by the joy of invention, imaginative people often fall into a seductive trap, stockpiling ideas without earning any cash. Nice work if you can get it, but only a few jobs are available in "Think Tanks".

"Get your first customer", is the golden rule when building a business. Customers will provide the cash to fund your future creativity.

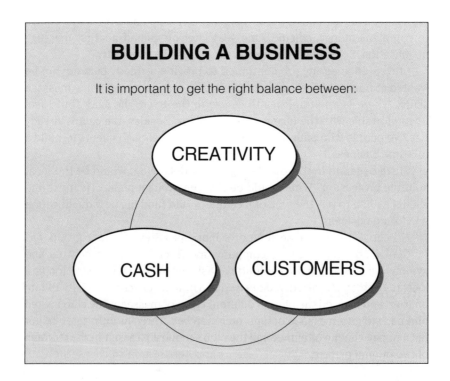

BUILDING A BUSINESS

It is important to get the right balance between:

CREATIVITY

CASH

CUSTOMERS

Paul Hawken reached millions of budding entrepreneurs with his American public television series *Growing a Business*. (His work is described in my book *The Art of Encouragement*, so those who have read it may want to skip the next page.) He speaks with authority, having built several successful businesses, starting with one of the first natural food stores in the USA. Based in Boston, the Erewhon Trading Company was grossing £25,000 a day in 1973. He later co-founded the mail-order firm Smith & Hawken. Located in Mill Valley, California, the company has built a reputation for delivering high-quality tools around the world. Paul believes strongly in small businesses, which play a key role in most nations' economies, and provides sound advice for people aiming to start their own firms.

Too much money is worse than too little

Businesses suffer from a lack of imagination, not capital, says Paul. Too much money tends to replace creativity. Companies without money are hungry; they must dream, imagine and improvise. Companies awash with money try to buy solutions. They lavish vast amounts on consultants, lawyers, clever accountants, publicity agents and marketing studies. Cash and creativity are both necessary, but make sure you balance them properly.

Cash management is a key skill in running a business. Stay in the black whenever possible. You need money? Double your efforts to find a new customer, rather than take a loan. Don't over-extend and pay vast sums to the bank manager. "Cash cows" are vital, maintaining the products and services which bring in the money.

Danish pastries may be your most profitable line, so keep selling them to the market. You feel bored and want to diversify? Make sure the Danish pastry business is running successfully, then appoint a champion to take it over. Hire somebody whose greatest desire in life is to sell Danish pastries. You can then experiment with other types of pastry. Cash tells the truth about a business, so dare to face the reality of the numbers. Build on what is working, not what you think "should work", and do more of these things. Increase your income and decrease your costs. Finally, pay your bills promptly, because other small businesses are relying on the money they get from you.

Re-create something that has been lost

People are attracted to nostalgia, so re-create something which they believe has been lost. The friendly small town bank; the reliable mail-order firm; the honest garage; the quality ice-cream shop; the traditional cheese store; the aromatic coffee shop; the company that fixes mistakes without complaint. Be honest, deliver quality and make people feel special.

"Remember that in business you are never trying to "beat" the competition," writes Paul. "You are trying to give your customers something other than what they are receiving from the competition. It is a waste of time and energy trying to beat the competition because the customer doesn't care about that rivalry.

Business will always have problems

Paul once searched for magic solutions. Providing he read more books by business gurus, he felt, one day he would find business nirvana. Enlightenment would make all his problems disappear. The truth hit him one sunny autumn afternoon:

"I had my nirvana, all right, but it was the opposite of what I had been seeking. On that pretty afternoon the actual truth finally struck me: I would always have problems. In fact, problems signify that the business is in a rapid learning phase. The revelation was liberating. I couldn't understand why other people hadn't told me this earlier."

Problems create either energy or paralysis, says Paul. Good managers make problems interesting and mobilise people's energies to find solutions. Bad managers present problems as threats, criticisms or things to be ignored. They issue memos, blame others or claim it is the customer's fault. Get used to problems, says Paul, they are an eternal part of everyday business life.

What is your strategy for success? What can you learn from good models who have achieved similar visions? How can you get the right balance between Creativity, Customers and Cash? Imagine you have achieved your vision. Looking back over the journey, what were the milestones on the road to success? The following pages offer exercises that you can use to clarify your strategy for achieving your vision.

● Successful strategies

"Do what works" is simple but sound advice when running a business. How do you discover what works? One way is to study people, teams or organisations that have reached similar goals to those that you want to achieve. Then take the following steps. First: Describe the results you want to achieve. Second: Describe the strategies that have worked before to achieve similar results. Third: Describe the things you can do to follow these strategies in your own way.

● Vision accomplished

This exercise is based on one described by Laurence G. Boldt in his book *Zen in the Art of Making a Living*. Imagine you have achieved your vision. Look back to how you made it happen. Describe: a) Your vision. b) The steps you took towards achieving your vision. c) The benefits of achieving your vision: for yourself, for other people and for the planet. Use the ideas you get from this exercise to create your strategy for achieving your vision.

● Building a business

Running a business calls for getting the right balance between Creativity, Customers and Cash. It is tempting to spend time developing creative ideas, for example, rather than getting customers who will provide the cash. Try the following exercise which is in three parts. Creativity: Describe your creative idea, product or service. Customers: Describe your first three customers. Cash: Describe your plans for gathering the cash. Getting funding will provide the life-blood to support your creativity.

● My strategy

Vision is the "What?", Strategy is the "How?". Start by writing each of your three main goals. Taking each one in turn, describe how you can reach the goals. Be as specific as possible. Providing you have got the "What?" right, the "How?" will be fairly obvious. The next step will be to translate the words into action and achieve your goals.

(Note: There is a similar exercise at the beginning of the next chapter. That exercise, called My Visible Results, invites you to be more specific about what you will do to achieve positive results. Tackle the exercise that you believe is most appropriate.)

● My milestones

Building a business, writing a book or completing any large task calls for successful project management. Begin by selecting the date by which you aim to reach your target. For example, imagine you want to accomplish a particular task within two years. Start from your destination and work backwards. Make a map showing the concrete things that must be happening at each stage of the journey. Take specific steps to pass each of these milestones and reach your target.

SUCCESSFUL STRATEGIES

"Do what works," is deceptively simple-sounding advice. How do you discover what works? One way is to study people, teams or organisations that have reached similar goals to those that you want to achieve. Then take the following steps. First: Describe the results you want to achieve. Second: Describe the strategies that have worked before to achieve similar results. Third: Describe the things you can do to follow these strategies in your own way.

The result I want to achieve is:

● To ....

**The strategies that have worked
before to achieve similar results are:**

● To ....

● To ....

● To ....

● To ....

● To ....

**The things I can do to follow
these strategies in my own way are:**

● To ....

● To ....

● To ....

VISION ACCOMPLISHED

Imagine you have achieved your vision. Look back to how you made it happen. Describe: a) Your vision. b) The steps you took towards achieving your vision. c) The benefits of achieving your vision: for yourself, for other people and for the planet. Use these ideas to create your strategy for achieving your vision.

My vision was:

●

The steps I took towards achieving my vision were:

●

●

●

●

●

The benefits of achieving my vision were:

●

●

●

BUILDING A BUSINESS

Building a business calls for getting the right balance between Creativity, Customers and Cash. It is tempting to spend time developing your creative ideas, for example, rather than getting customers who will provide the cash. Try the following exercise.

CREATIVITY

My creative idea, service or product Is:

● ....

....

CUSTOMERS

My first three customers are:

● ....

● ....

● ....

CASH

My plans for getting enough cash are:

● ....

● ....

● ....

MY STRATEGY: THE "HOW?"

Vision is the "What?"; Strategy is the "How?". First: Write each of your three main goals. Make sure you focus on the real results you want to achieve. Second: Write how you can do your best to achieve each of these results. You may wish to brainstorm lots of "Hows?", prioritise the ideas and then make a specific action plan.

(Please note: There is a similar exercise at the beginning of the next chapter. That exercise, called *My Visible Results,* invites you to be more specific about what you will do to achieve positive results. Tackle the exercise that you believe is most appropriate.)

My first goal: The real result I want to achieve is:

1) To ....

My strategy: The things I can do to
do my best to achieve this result are:

● To ....

● To ....

● To ....

● To ....

● To ....

My second goal: The real result I want to achieve is:

2) To ....

My strategy: The things I can do to
do my best to achieve this result are:

●   To ....

●   To ....

●   To ....

●   To ....

●   To ....

My third goal: The real result I want to achieve is:

3) To ....

My strategy: The things I can do to
do my best to achieve this result are:

●   To ....

●   To ....

●   To ....

●   To ....

●   To ....

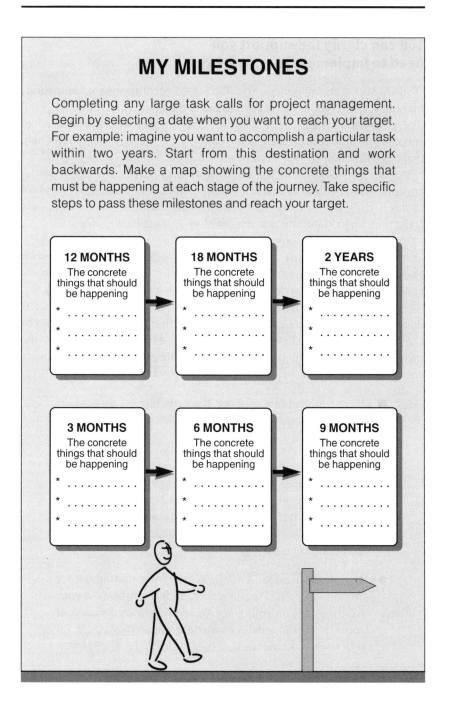

MY MILESTONES

Completing any large task calls for project management. Begin by selecting a date when you want to reach your target. For example: imagine you want to accomplish a particular task within two years. Start from this destination and work backwards. Make a map showing the concrete things that must be happening at each stage of the journey. Take specific steps to pass these milestones and reach your target.

12 MONTHS
The concrete things that should be happening
* . . . .
* . . . .
* . . . .

18 MONTHS
The concrete things that should be happening
* . . . .
* . . . .
* . . . .

2 YEARS
The concrete things that should be happening
* . . . .
* . . . .
* . . . .

3 MONTHS
The concrete things that should be happening
* . . . .
* . . . .
* . . . .

6 MONTHS
The concrete things that should be happening
* . . . .
* . . . .
* . . . .

9 MONTHS
The concrete things that should be happening
* . . . .
* . . . .
* . . . .

You can clarify the support you
need to implement your strategy

"You are such a strong person. You don't need encouragement," somebody may tell you. Everybody needs help to climb their particular mountain, even if it is limited to buying a reliable rope. People who are starved of encouragement freeze on the glacier. Creating a good support plan can help them to reach their chosen summit.

Artists face tough challenges finding backing in the commercial world, says Eric Maisel in *Staying Sane in the Arts*. Painters, sculptors and writers love to stay in the studio and may find difficulty negotiating with reality. Solitude is the time when many artists feel most alive. Eric explains:

"In the bubble of absorption that is the most precious aspect of solitude, artists can be together with their love — their medium, their art, their work. They can connect with melody, meter or colour. They wake up dreaming about the work they'll get done in the solitude that each new day brings."

Solitude is a time when artists meet their destiny. But being alone has its drawbacks. Emerging to face people, they may find their work is rejected by the world. Sometimes they must listen to suggestions, face the truth and improve. Sometimes the buyers are simply being fickle. How to deal with such setbacks? Eric Maisel's advice includes the following tips:

- Have a marketable product. If you do highly personal art that has a questionable chance of reaching an audience, diversify.

- Disidentify from your product. You are not your painting, novel or performance. When your agent says that your novel is not working for him, he is really talking about your novel. He is not calling you incompetent or a failure. Be able to step aside and hear what your agent, your director or the curator is saying.

- Acquire advocates. A room is less intimidating with a friendly face in it. People who have already bought your paintings are on your side. An agent who sold a book of yours is on your side. A playwright whose play you lit up with your performance is on your side. You may approach these people with confidence.

- Prepare for business events. Rehearse. Ask yourself potential questions and answer them. Meet potential objections. Role-play with a friend, your partner or your therapist.

- Strive to gain a small audience, even an audience of one. Has someone responded to your work? Has someone advocated your work and sought to advance you? Re-establish and maintain contact with those important persons. Invite them to a private showing of your new work. Cultivate a relationship with, and make time for, anyone who respects your work.

Strong people also need help to reach their goals. Christina Noble pays generous tribute to Dr O'Connell, a counsellor. He helped her to lay the ghosts of the past and to generate the strengths required to pursue her vocation.

Matt Busby needed contributions from the board of directors, training staff and players to realise his goals at Manchester United.

Anita Roddick enlisted the financial talents of Gordon, her husband, to take care of economic matters at the Body Shop. Few people achieve their vision without assistance from anybody.

How can you get encouragement? Try tackling the exercise called My Support. First: Write the names of people whose assistance you need to implement your strategy. For example: your family, friends, colleagues, managers, suppliers and customers. Second: Write the practical, financial or emotional support you want from these people. Third: Write the specific things you can do to gain their support .

Building on what you have written, tackle the exercise called My Support Network. Draw a map showing the people — and other things — that give you support. Describe the support they each provide. Somebody on a Career Development workshop drew a map showing over 50 people, two dogs, his record collection and the local football team. Encouragement is a two-way process, of course, so find ways to support your Encouragers.

"I want to pursue a creative idea in my company. How can I get backing to make it happen?" you may ask. Win your "sponsors". The people whose permission, practical help and support you need to bring your idea to fruition. Sponsors may include, for example, the chief executive, managers and key colleagues. Decision makers often tend to be conservative. They will only support a new idea if, in their view of the world, it has at least a 9/10 chance of guaranteed success. How to get their backing? When putting forward your suggestion, show people how introducing it:

a) Will be profitable.

b) Will be practical.

c) Will be virtually guaranteed
to produce positive results.

Sally, a sales manager, faced a tough challenge when seeking backing from her sponsors. They were the finance director, the I.T. director and the chief executive. How to sell her suggestion for improving what the company offered to customers? The problem was compounded by each person having a different "buying style".

The finance director only accepted an idea if it was written on a memo, was safe and cost little money. The sales director only accepted an idea if it was pioneering, a bit crazy and reflected well on the sales office. The chief executive did not like memos. He only accepted an idea if you went to him with your first customer. Sally kept her honesty but also found different ways to show the benefits to each sponsor. Getting the first customer also proved her idea could boost the company's bottom line.

How can you win support from your sponsors? Try tackling two exercises on this theme, the first is called My Sponsors. Do three things: First: Write the names of people from whom you want sponsorship, permission and support to pursue your idea. Second: Write the type of support you want from each of these people. Third: Write the specific things you can do to get their sponsorship.

Building on these themes, move to the next exercise called Selling To My Sponsors. Decision makers prefer suggestions that have at least a 9/10 chance of achieving success. Describe how you can show people that pursuing your idea: a) Will be profitable. b) Will be practical. c) Will be virtually guaranteed to achieve positive results. Then go ahead and sell your idea to your sponsors.

"I make the best action plans in the world, but find it hard to translate the words into action. How do you get started?" asked a participant on a Career Development workshop. Seeing is believing, so always plan how to get some early wins. Success generates the confidence to climb towards your chosen summit. Let's explore how to implement your strategy and achieve your vision.

MY SUPPORT

What help do you need to implement your strategy? First: Write the names of people from whom you need support. Second: Write the kind of help you want from them. Third: Write what you can do to win their support. (This page only provides space for one person, but you may wish to complete the exercise elsewhere.)

The person's name:

● ....

The support I would like from this person is:

● ....

● ....

● ....

The specific things I can do to get support from this person are:

● ....

● ....

● ....

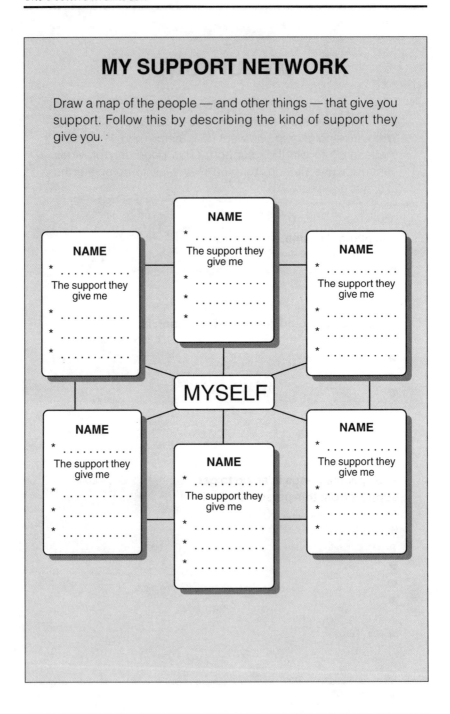

MY SUPPORT NETWORK

Draw a map of the people — and other things — that give you support. Follow this by describing the kind of support they give you.

MY SPONSORS

Write three things: First: The names of people from whom you want sponsorship, permission and support to pursue your idea. Second: The type of support you want from each person. Third: The specific things you can do to get sponsorship from each person.

The sponsor:

● ....

The support I want from this sponsor is:

● ....

● ....

● ....

**The specific things I can do to
get support from this sponsor are:**

● ....

● ....

● ....

SELLING TO MY SPONSORS

Describe the concrete things you can do
to show that pursuing your suggestion

a) Will be profitable:

●   I can ....

●   I can ....

●   I can ....

b) Will be practical:

●   I can ....

●   I can ....

●   I can ....

c) Will be virtually guaranteed
   to produce positive results:

●   I can ....

●   I can ....

●   I can ....

Step Three:
VISIBLE RESULTS

CHERYL SCHOFIELD is somebody who produces visible results. A 40-year-old Lancastrian dynamo, she revolutionises hospitals in the private sector. Patients, staff and employers hold her in high regard. She improves the quality of care, inspires the staff to do their best and boosts the profit.

"What is your purpose in life?", I asked her out of the blue one day. She replied without pausing: "To help people to make life better for themselves." She has a combination of ideals demonstrated by many people who do work they love. Driven by strong values, she also thrives in the commercial world.

A nurse by training, Cheryl gives the staff clear signals when she is invited to manage a hospital. "The first signal is that everything must be geared to caring for the patients," she says. Money is invested in equipment to provide top-class health care. "The second signal is that the staff's know-how will be recognised and used," continues Cheryl.

Old hospitals were often organised to suit the doctors and nurses. She encourages the staff to produce ideas for putting patients first and improving the working environment. Introducing their suggestions provides two quick wins. Staff see their ideas are valued and the patients also benefit. "Change the physical things to change the psychological things," is an old adage. Cheryl produces early visible results to show people she means business.

"The third signal is that we must pay our way in the world," says Cheryl. "Staff may find this hard to stomach, but it is a reality." Money is spent on presenting a professional image, such as good uniforms, redecorating the hospital and making the grounds attractive. Money is invested in marketing to attract patients. "We cannot offer all treatments to everybody," says Cheryl. "We concentrate on our strengths and show the quality of our care to potential patients."

During the past five years she has helped to turn around three small private hospitals. "Staff do the real work," says Cheryl. "I provide the structure which allows them to follow their mission. Like all nurses and doctors, we simply want to care for the patients."

Alec Dickson has also inspired many people to produce visible results. Reporting as a journalist for *The Daily Telegraph* in 1938, he put down his pen to aid Czech refugees, smuggling many to safety in Britain. He spent the next 20 years creating self-help projects in Europe and Africa, before founding Voluntary Service Overseas in 1958.

Martin Garner, one of the first volunteers, describes Alec as "a whirlwind of energy, an attempter of the impossible, with the genius of inspiring others". He recalls his first "interview" with him in the book *Arriving Where We*

Started. Travelling up to London, he sought Alec's backing to do volunteer work in Sarawak.

"His home, in Mortlake, was knee-deep in papers — correspondence, newspaper cuttings and books in the making were everywhere. I didn't know how to cross the room to the snowed-in chair I was offered. The lighting was dim and the décor dark; I had the distinct feeling that I was in the jungle already.

"But Alec Dickson was no fumbler in the dark; he knew exactly where he was going. He talked quickly, with fire in his eye, once leaping across the room reliving a party in Nigeria where he had sung: 'Daisy, Daisy give me your answer do', slapping his bottom as he rode his imaginary bicycle made for two.

"Undisputed Queen of this Thames-side bedlam was Mora, Alec's wife. She seemed oblivious to it all, the perfect county hostess, handing me a cup of tea and chunks of delicious home-made fruit cake: I was, after all, but a schoolboy . . . "

Alec gave many such young people the opportunity to build a better world. Voluntary Service Overseas had two objectives:

- To build up the self-reliance, self-respect and self-generating resources of the people in the countries to which the volunteers are posted.

- To build up here in the United Kingdom an understanding about the reality of the world in which we are all a part.

V.S.O. became a model for the U.S. Peace Corps, but Alec felt restless. Every morning he opened the newspaper to see social problems in Britain, writes Mora Dickson in A *Chance To Serve*. Alec's genius was to weld together two factors. First: the unmet needs in society. Second: the idealism of young people. Why not tackle the first problem by channelling the youngsters' desire to improve society? The result was Community Service Volunteers. Created in 1962, it gave young people the chance to serve others in a mental hospital, adventure playground, reform institution, housing estate, or wherever. C.S.V. was built on three principles:

- That young people want to feel needed.

- That opportunities for service can be found on our own doorsteps.

● That we should search for situations where the contribution of young people will be valuable precisely because they are young people.

"No volunteer should ever be rejected," was a basic principle of C.S.V., a belief which was soon put to the test. Mora writes: "The first blind girl found her way to Alec Dickson's door to tell him she had been refused by every other volunteer organisation in Britain but she was determined, somehow, to get herself off the receiving end of help and start giving. It was the acid test of the principle of 'no person is ever refused'."

Alec weaved past bureaucratic obstacles to find a place where the girl could use her talents. C.S.V. still offers volunteering opportunities to the young, old, able-bodied, disabled, police, offenders and people from all walks of life.

"Everybody has something to give." said Alec. "But the giver also learns by giving. One volunteer returned from India to report he was the person whose life had been enriched." Right up to his death in 1994, Alec continued to travel the world. Why? "Are there no longer any unmet needs in modern society?" he asked. Nobody who is ill, nobody who is lonely, nobody whose life cannot be uplifted by human contact?

The world is full of problems, but there are millions of people who want to implement solutions. Volunteering can help, but one day we must all take our responsibility. Alec said: "There comes a point when you can't pay people to do your loving for you." His visible results go far beyond creating V.S.O. and C.S.V. Alec's legacy lives on through thousands of former volunteers who are striving to build a better world.

How hungry are you to do work you enjoy? People have different reasons for pursuing their calling. They may aim to feed their family, use their talents or improve the planet. Eric Maisel maintains that love is the spirit that motivates the artist's journey. The love may be sublime, raw, obsessive, passionate, awful, or thrilling, but whatever its quality, it is a powerful motive in the artist's life. Eric describes how Derek Jacobi, the actor, distinguished this special drive from mere desire:

"You have to have an absolute obsession and compulsion to act, not just desire; it's just not enough to have talent and want to express it; it's not enough. It's got to be more deeply rooted, more abrasive. The fire in the belly has got to be there. If there's no fire, you can't do it."

Time to make a decision. Try tackling the following exercise which explores how motivated you are to pursue your vocation.

● Am I serious?

How serious are you about doing work you love? Consider the sacrifices and challenges on the route to achieving your vision. What will be the pluses and minuses? What will be the pluses and minuses of not doing work you love? Bearing these things in mind, rate how serious you are on the scale 0 — 10. Be honest when giving a rating. You may be better suited to following some other path. One point worth considering: People who succeed in doing work they love rate themselves as at least a 9 out of 10.

AM I SERIOUS?

● Take a moment to think about the hard work and challenges to be overcome on the way to achieving your vision. Bearing these things in mind:

● How serious are you about doing work you love?

● Rate how serious you are on the scale 0 —10 below.

| 0 | 1 | 2 | 3 | 4 | 5 | 6 | 7 | 8 | 9 | 10 |

You can do the work

Peter Vidmar, who won the Gymnastic Gold Medal at the 1984 Los Angeles Olympics, describes how people can work to achieve Peak Performance. (His story was included in my book *The Art of Encouragement*, so you may wish to skip it if you have read that book.) He tells conference audiences that gymnasts must first achieve the Olympic Standard of performance to gain a mark of 9.4. They can then add 0.2 by taking a Risk, 0.2 by demonstrating Originality and 0.2 by showing Virtuosity. This produces a perfect 10 and wins them the Olympic Gold.

Many people leave the speech feeling inspired, saying: "We can now believe in our dreams, take risks and go for it." They forget Peter's most important message: he said that people must first achieve the 9.4. They must work to reach the Olympic Standard in their chosen walk of life, profession or business.

Peak Performers work hard to achieve the 9.4. They do the right thing in the right way every day. Jack Nicklaus, the golfer, began each season by practising his driving, chipping and putting. Great singers, dancers, actors, engineers, sports teams, organisations and companies continually focus on getting the basics right. They practise inner discipline, enjoy the journey and reach the 9.4. Peak Performers practise so that they can forget. They then relax and go for the perfect 10.

What is the 9.4 in your business? How can you achieve your 10? Try tackling the next exercise which focuses on getting the basics right and going on to reach your goals.

● My visible results

How can you translate your vision into visible results? Taking each goal in turn, brainstorm all the practical things you must do to translate your vision into reality. Take heart if you produce a long list of actions. Build in some early successes and make plans for encouraging yourself on the journey. Providing you keep doing the right things every day, you will achieve your vision.

It's time to do the work, but prepare for a few contradictions. Sweat is required, but it won't be all labour. People who pursue their vocation often mix work and play. Identify the tasks to be completed, then relax. You may find it rewarding to follow three principles when tackling the tasks. First: To follow your successful patterns. Second: To make the most of your prime times. Third: To give yourself energy to complete the journey. Let's explore each of these principles.

Follow your successful patterns. Everybody has rich seams of past achievements, but they often ignore this gold mine. You may recall the exercise called My Creative Times. You remembered what you did well to perform creative work by yourself, in a team or in an organisation. Keep doing what works. Pursue your successful patterns to produce visible results. Building on this principle, let's explore how to make good use of your day.

Make the best use of your prime times. Everybody has prime times when they feel inspired to do creative work. My best time for writing, for example, is in the morning between 8.30 and 12.00. Writing in *The Ageless Spirit*, Rollo May described how he chose to protect his precious hours.

MY VISIBLE RESULTS

Begin by writing your three main goals. Follow this by describing the specific things you must do to achieve each of these goals. Tick off the items as you complete the action steps and achieve your successes.

MY FIRST GOAL IS:

● ....

**The specific things I must do
to achieve this goal are:**

● ....

● ....

● ....

● ....

● ....

MY SECOND GOAL IS:

● ....

The specific things I must do to achieve this goal are:

● ....

● ....

● ....

● ....

● ....

MY THIRD GOAL IS:

● ....

The specific things I must do to achieve this goal are:

● ....

● ....

● ....

● ....

● ....

How do you protect your prime times? Structure your day to capitalise on these fertile hours. Sometimes this calls for being tough. Give clear messages to people that you will see them at another time during the day. Sounds hard? "Catch the wave" is the motto. Missing the wave means it has gone for ever, never to return.

My Prime Times is an exercise which invites you to identify and make good use of such times. First: Describe your shorter prime times, for example, a particular time of the day when you work best. Second: Describe your longer prime times, for example, a longer period of time when you work best. You may perform best when setting aside a block of time, such as a month or so, to tackle a project. Alternatively, you may perform best during a particular season of the year. Third: Describe the practical things you can do in order to create and make the best of both your shorter and longer prime times.

How do you give yourself energy? Cars need fuel to cross a desert; people need "fuel" to pursue their personal journeys. My Energy Givers is an exercise which explores methods for charging your batteries. People get stimulation from different sources. Some play music or walk in the woods; some spend time with Encouragers or work at a certain spot in the house. Describe the activities, people and other stimulating things that generate energy.

My Best Working Day invites you to build on these ideas and design your perfect working day. Remember your Successful Patterns, Prime Times and Energy Givers. Capitalise on these to complete the necessary daily tasks and get some visible successes. Use the page to write or draw your best day. (Perhaps you have different types of days. One day when you work at home, for example, another day when you are on the road. So it may be useful to design different types of perfect days.)

"Rising from your bed in the morning, you must face an empty page," said Joan, my writing teacher from Antioch College. "Writers experience one of three kinds of days: Great Days, Good Days and Graft Days." Great Days are when you flow, fly and feel alive. Words flow easily on to the page. Discovering fresh ideas, you explore new lands. Good Days are when you perform a competent job. You then feel satisfied at the end of the day. Graft Days remind you of pushing water uphill. You slog away, tackle even the grim tasks and encourage yourself.

"Anybody can work on a Great Day," argued Joan. "But professional writers also get things done on a Graft Day." Similar rules apply in other fields, so make sure you can manage the different kinds of creative days.

THE CREATIVE DAYS

People need to manage different kinds of days when performing creative work. They may experience, for example:

● GREAT DAYS

These are the days when:
- You flow.
- You fly.
- You feel alive.
- You discover new things.
- You feel totally creative.

● GOOD DAYS

These are the days when:
- You focus.
- You work well.
- You feel encouraged.
- You feel satisfied at the end of the day.
- You finish what you aimed to do.

● GRAFT DAYS

These are the days when:
- You feel as if you are pushing water uphill.
- You keep slogging.
- You even tackle the grim tasks.
- You encourage yourself.
- You get things done even on a graft day.

MY PRIME TIMES

Everybody has prime times when they feel inspired to do creative work. This exercise invites you to identify and make good use of such times. First: Describe your shorter prime times; for example, a particular time of the day when you work best. Second: Describe your longer prime times, for example, a longer period of time when you work best. You may perform best when setting aside a block of time, such as a month or so, to tackle a project. Alternatively, you may perform best during a particular season of the year. Third: Describe the practical things you can do to create and make the best of both your shorter and longer prime times.

My shorter prime times are:

● ....

● ....

● ....

My longer prime times are:

● ....

● ....

● ....

MAKING THE BEST
OF MY PRIME TIMES

List the practical things you can do to create and make the best of your Prime Times.

**How I can create and make the
best use of my shorter Prime Times:**

- ....
- ....
- ....

**How I can create and make the
best use of my longer Prime Times:**

- ....
- ....
- ....

MY ENERGY GIVERS

People get energy from different sources. Some play music or walk in the woods; some spend time with Encouragers or work at a certain spot in the house. Describe the activities, people and other stimulating things that generate energy.

The things that give me energy are:

- ....
  ....

- ....
  ....

- ....
  ....

- ....
  ....

- ....
  ....

MY BEST WORKING DAY

This exercise invites you to design your perfect working day. Remember your Successful Patterns, Prime Times and Energy Givers. Capitalise on these to complete the necessary daily tasks and get some visible successes. Use the page to write or draw your best day. (Perhaps you have different types of days. One day when you work at home, for example, another day when you are on the road. So it may be useful to design different types of perfect days.)

My best working day is:

You can do superb quality work

How can you give quality service to your customers? Banks, hotels, shops and many other businesses have suffered a rude awakening during the last decade. Satisfying customers is no longer optional; it is a requirement in today's world. Why go that extra mile to provide superb service? Apart from making financial sense, it is also moral. Customers are the people who pay your wages. Try tackling this well-known exercise which explores your own experience as a customer.

● Good service

First: Think of a good service you have received. For example: in a restaurant, shop, travel company, hotel or public service. Write the name of the organisation. Second: Write what people did right to give good service. For example: they greeted me warmly; they remembered my name; they gave me their full attention; they solved my problem immediately; they phoned one week later to ensure everything was satisfactory. Third: Describe the specific things you can do to give good service to your customers.

Quality calls for giving people what they expect. You have certain expectations, for example, when staying at an average-priced hotel: a friendly welcome; a clean room; a colour television; a telephone; room service; reasonable food; quick check-out; etc. Good hotels go beyond getting these basics right, they also provide excellent service. How? They do that little bit extra to make the customer feel valued. The receptionist, for example, may offer to book rail or air tickets for you to pick up later in the day. What will you recall from your visit? Assuming the hotel got the basics right, you will remember the human touch. How do you give people quality service? Whatever your business, you will find it rewarding:

a) To give people what they expect.

b) To give people "a little bit more" than they expect.

"But won't I go bankrupt?" somebody may ask. You obviously do not give a customer a Rolls-Royce when they ordered a Volkswagen. Giving the bit extra seldom involves money. It often involves somebody — a receptionist, waiter or cleaner — showing they care. Bear one further thought in mind. "Today's luxury becomes tomorrow's expectation." Customers expect consistent treatment whenever they visit a shop, fly an airline or pay for a

GOOD SERVICE

a) Think of a service you have received which was good. This may have been from a restaurant, shop, travel organisation, hotel or a public service. Write the name of the organisation.

....

b) Describe the specific things that people did right to provide good service.

● They ....

● They ....

● They ....

● They ....

● They ....

c) How can you follow these steps in your own way? Describe the specific things that you can do to give good service to your customers.

● I can ....

● I can ....

● I can ....

meal. A restaurant may offer diners an After Eight chocolate to accompany their coffee, for example, but woe betide the restaurant if it fails to give this "little bit extra" on their next visit. Why offer quality service? Because business becomes even more enjoyable. People also remember the human touch. They provide repeat business and recommend you to friends.

Imagine you run a small Italian restaurant. How can you offer superb service to your customers? One approach is to improve the Four Ps in the total service package: the Products, People-skills, Procedures and Packaging. Barrie Hopson and Mike Scally expand on this model in their book *Twelve Steps To Success Through Service*. Let's explore how to apply these ideas in the Italian restaurant. (Later you will be invited to tackle an exercise applying similar methods to your own business.)

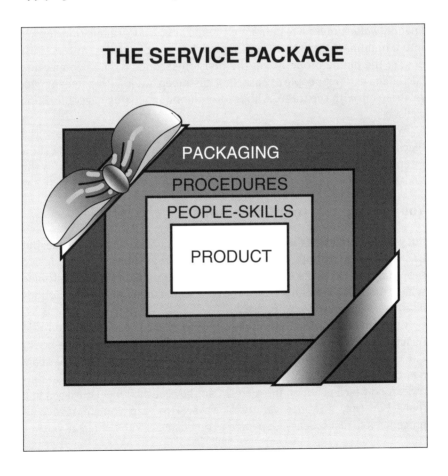

THE SERVICE PACKAGE

PACKAGING

PROCEDURES

PEOPLE-SKILLS

PRODUCT

You can improve your Products

Delicious Italian food is the starting point. Smiling waiters won't win the customers if the food tastes awful. The contrast between the friendly waiters and bad food might make them even angrier. Quality products are the starting point. Get the basics right with a clean, attractive restaurant, a range of good Italian food and reasonable prices.

Building on these foundations, continually improve your products. Provide a wider range of Italian desserts, for example, but never diversify at the cost of spoiling your original quality product. Offer the right product in the right way every day to satisfy your customers.

You can improve your People-skills

Friendly waiters make a restaurant visit enjoyable; rude waiters transform it into a nightmare. Staff must use appropriate people-skills. Waiters must answer the phone properly, get the first ten seconds right when greeting customers and put people at ease. Few customers want a deep, meaningful relationship with the waiter who is intent upon practising his counselling skills.

What are appropriate people-skills? It depends on your business. The teacher must use more people-skills than the plumber, but both must show interest in helping their customers. What skills should staff show in the Italian restaurant? How can you help them to improve their people-skills?

You can improve your Procedures

Put your customers first rather than last. Sounds like commercial sense. But banks, hotels and shops often opt for "customer prevention". They design procedures to make life easy for themselves but difficult for the customer. When somebody gets angry, they reply: "It is company policy and nobody else has complained."

Customers want to give you their money. Make it easy for them to do business with you. Can they easily find your restaurant in the phone-book? Can they phone any time of day? Can they easily book a table? Can they park nearby? Can they relax in a comfortable place to wait for a table? Can they order food which is not on the menu? Can they get their meal quickly if in a rush? Can they pay in a variety of ways? How can you improve your procedures to make it easy for people to do business with the restaurant?

You can improve your Packaging

Packaging calls for presenting your products and services in a way that is attractive to the customers. People see your business from the outside in. They notice the advertisements in the telephone book; the restaurant's appearance; the music; the menu; the waiter's uniform; the food on the plate. Perception is reality in the customer's world.

Sometimes this is unfair. Diners who see spots on the menu think you neglect cleanliness and have cockroaches crawling in the kitchen. Staff must train themselves to see things through the customer's eyes. How can you improve the packaging?

Return to your own business. How can you improve your total Service Package? Tackle the exercises on the next few pages called My Products, My People-skills, My Procedures and My Packaging. The four areas merge together, especially in the caring professions. But use the model to create fresh ideas for improving your restaurant, shop, aerobics class, training consultancy or whatever. Performing superb work will generate some future business, but sometimes you must devote time and money to sales and marketing. Let's explore these techniques for attracting customers.

MY PRODUCTS

Describe three concrete ways you can improve the products and services that you offer to your customers.

1) I can ....

....

2) I can ....

....

3) I can ....

....

MY PEOPLE-SKILLS

Describe three concrete ways you can improve the people-skills involved in delivering good service to your customers. This can also include people-management inside your organisation.

1)   I can ....

     ....

2)   I can ....

     ....

3)   I can ....

     ....

MY PROCEDURES

Describe three concrete ways you can improve the procedures really to put the customers first and make it easy for them to do business with you.

1)   I can ....

     ....

2)   I can ....

     ....

3)   I can ....

     ....

MY PACKAGING

Describe three concrete ways you can improve the way you present your products and services to your customers.

1) I can ....

....

2) I can ....

....

3) I can ....

....

You can improve your sales and marketing

"I find it difficult to build my business," said Claire, a former physical education instructor, who specialised in running outdoor training activities on Dartmoor. "Partly I find it hard to sell myself. Partly I feel exhausted after three days spent hiking over the moors. I write the bills and catch up on the post, but it is then time to prepare for the next programme. Business is ticking over, but I face the same weekly grind for the next few years. I do not have time or energy to call potential clients and expand the company."

Claire faced the dilemma confronting many small businesses. She *was* the business. Three part-time assistants helped with rock-climbing, canoeing, safety and office chores, but customers bought her expertise. Oil, electricity and engineering firms had despatched graduates to Dartmoor over the years as part of their induction training. "Outward Bound" programmes proliferated on the market, but old customers bought a guaranteed result when hiring Claire.

She now faced a life-shaping decision. "Do I want to run a small business or do I want to expand?" Pluses and minuses abounded on both sides. If she wanted to expand, however, she must sell more programmes.

The classic "Sales Funnel" held the key for Claire (see illustration on a later page). Increasing revenue called for getting the right people to do the right things at each stage of the funnel. The five stages were:

1) Reaching the customers.

2) Meeting the customers.

3) Agreeing business with the customers.

4) Giving good service to the customers.

5) Getting repeat business from the customers.

Reaching more customers was a top priority. Cold calling on the telephone seldom sells training, so Claire must explore other ways to reach decision makers. Personal recommendations stood most chance of success, but she also fancied writing articles and displaying at exhibitions. The same challenge confronts many small businesses.

How to reach potential customers? Writing in *Making a Living Without a Job*, Barbara Winter includes some of the following methods for "Marketing on a Shoestring".

* Advertising
* Articles
* Brochures
* Business cards
* Conference speaking
* Customer newsletters
* Direct mailing
* Exhibitions
* Networking
* Niche marketing
* Personal contacts
* Presentations
* Product demonstrations
* Publicity

Claire faced another dilemma. She sold her time and only got paid for hiking on the moors. Stage One of the Sales Funnel called for reaching new customers. This meant setting aside at least five days a month, cutting the money-earning days. Stages Two and Three posed a greater financial challenge. Companies now asked for training activities to be tailored to meet their needs.

Claire could satisfy clients by providing outdoor adventures that were 20 per cent customised and 80 per cent based on core programmes. The 20 per cent called for travelling to the South East, however, to meet decision-makers. Claire altered her policy of never charging for client meetings. Pitching for business must still be free. But she began charging clients half the daily training rate when meeting to finalise customised programmes for their staff. Stage Four of the Sales Funnel was Claire's favourite: she enjoyed giving good service to her customers, which often produced repeat business.

How to move the company forward? Claire had three choices. First: To be content and retain the status quo. Second: To remain a small company but significantly increase her fees. Third: To build a bigger business. The third option meant hiring more people to reach customers, meet customers and deliver training activities.

Claire chose the second option. Getting quotes from loyal customers, she published articles in training magazines, attended exhibitions and spoke at conferences. Two years later she wrote a book on outdoor training. Trading on her credibility as an author, she further increased her client fees. Claire preferred to work with a few people, rather than manage a large business. She chose the route that best suited her personality and boosted her finances.

How can you attract more customers? Try tackling the exercise called The Sales Funnel. Describe the concrete things that you, or your colleagues, can do at each stage of the sales process. How can you reach customers, meet customers, agree business with customers, deliver good service to customers and get repeat business with customers? Make sure you have the right people doing the right things at each successive stage of the sales funnel.

Selling products, for example, doesn't always require the managing director to spend days ringing to get appointments. You might hire telesales people, employ direct mailing and place newspaper advertisements. How can you sell more business?

People choose different ways to market their skills. Methods include: brochures, presentations, conference speeches, customer newsletters, articles, books, cold calls and keeping in touch with top customers. There is no right or wrong way. The only criteria is: Does it work?

Try tackling the series of exercises collected together under the title of My Marketing Plan. (The eight exercises are rewarding but take time. Choose those most relevant to your business.) You may prefer to skip this part and move on to the next section, however, which explores how to be a good finisher.

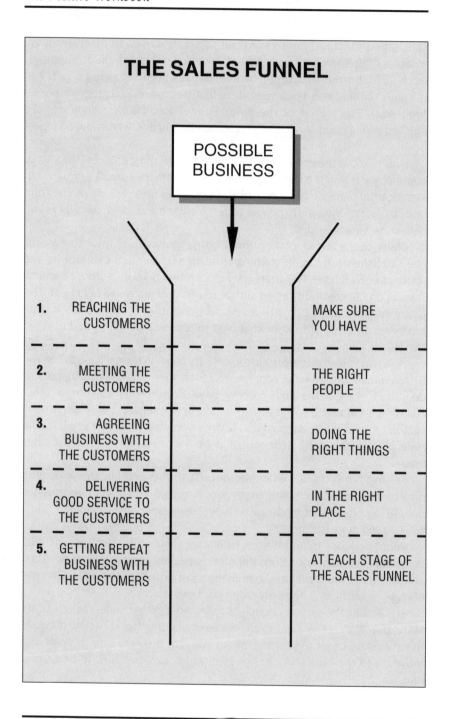

THE SALES FUNNEL

POSSIBLE BUSINESS

1. REACHING THE CUSTOMERS

MAKE SURE YOU HAVE

2. MEETING THE CUSTOMERS

THE RIGHT PEOPLE

3. AGREEING BUSINESS WITH THE CUSTOMERS

DOING THE RIGHT THINGS

4. DELIVERING GOOD SERVICE TO THE CUSTOMERS

IN THE RIGHT PLACE

5. GETTING REPEAT BUSINESS WITH THE CUSTOMERS

AT EACH STAGE OF THE SALES FUNNEL

THE SALES FUNNEL

Describe the concrete things you, or your colleagues, can do at each stage of the sales funnel.

How I/we can reach the customers:

- ....
- ....
- ....

How I/we can meet the customers:

- ....
- ....
- ....

How I/we can agree business with the customers:

- ....
- ....
- ....

How I/we can give good service to the customers:

- ....
- ....
- ....

How I/we can get repeat business with the customers:

- ....
- ....
- ....

How I/we can make sure the right people are doing the right things in the right way at each stage of the sales funnel:

- ....
- ....
- ....

MY MARKETING PLAN

● My top customers: How to give them special attention

Do you already have customers? If so, start with this exercise. The 80/20 rule says that 80 per cent of our business comes from 20 per cent of our customers. It makes sense to identify and keep in touch with these people who pay the bulk of your wages. First: List the names of your top customers. Second: List the specific things you can do to give special attention to each of these top customers. You may win so much repeat business that you do not need any further marketing plan.

● My marketing style

"I'm no good at marketing because I hate cold calling on the telephone," somebody may say. But there are many ways to perform successful marketing. What is your preferred style? You may like to speak at conferences, write articles, network through friends, display at exhibitions, give free presentations or whatever. The proof of the pudding is in the eating. Does it work?

Market in the way that feels right for you, but also make sure it produces results. What if it doesn't? Earn enough money to hire somebody who is brilliant. Make sure they go beyond presenting fancy concepts, however; pay them when they produce customers.

● My network

People buy products or services, but in fact they often choose to buy from a particular person. They hire somebody they know, somebody others recommend or somebody who has a good reputation. Personal recommendation is the best advertisement and people often buy through networks.

As a seller, how big is your network? Who do you know who might buy your products or services? Who do you know who has contacts? "I don't know anybody," somebody may say. Most individuals know at least 300 other people by name. Draw a map of your personal network. Start with the people you know best, plus any customers, then expand your map. List everybody who might buy your products or put you in touch with potential customers.

● My customers' wants

Good marketing starts from the customers' point of view. Who are your key customers? Get inside their skin and understand their agenda. What do they want? Most people want to be happy and successful, but they express these desires in a thousand different ways. First: Write a list of your customers. Second: Write what each of these customers wants. Be as specific as possible.

● My customers' buying style

How do your customers buy things? Managing directors will often give only 10 seconds of their time to listening to anybody who pitches for business. The seller must speak in headlines and show how their product will boost the company's profits. People who buy chewing gum often pick up the gum at the so-called "hot spots" in shops, such as near the check-out counter in the supermarket.

People who are searching for counselling help may consult the local Yellow Pages or, more likely, find help via a friend, doctor or crisis centre. First: Write a list of your customers. Second: Describe how each of these customers buys things.

● My products: The customer benefits

"What's in it for me?" asks the customer. People buy things which they feel will improve their life or work. Seen from the customer's point of view, why should they buy what you offer? First: Describe the products and services that you offer to your customers. Second: Describe the benefits they will gain from buying what you offer. Be as specific as possible. How will the products or services you offer help people to achieve their goals in life or work?

● My marketing channels

Earlier we looked at your preferred marketing style, but will such activities bear fruit? Will you reach key decision makers? Recalling their buying style: What is the best way to reach your potential customers? Personal introduction, direct mail, advertising, presentations, exhibitions or some other method? Whatever channel you use, how can you stand out from the crowd? Describe how to reach potential customers and grab their attention.

● My marketing plan

Building on what you have written, create your marketing plan. Remember these points when developing your plan: a) Your top customers. b) Your network. c) Your preferred marketing style. d) Your customers' wants. e) Your customers' buying style. f) Your products and the customer benefits. g) Your marketing channels. Be selective to be effective. Describe three specific things you can do to market what you offer and reach potential customers. Build in some early successes.

Marketing can become a religion in itself, so get the right balance. Set aside time to do the actual work that earns the money. The best marketing is quality work, satisfied customers and a superb reputation. This calls for being a good finisher. Let's explore how you can finally achieve your vision.

MY TOP CUSTOMERS:
How I can give them special attention

The 80/20 rule says that 80 per cent of our business comes from 20 per cent of our customers. So it makes sense to identify and keep in touch with these people. List the names of your top customers and how you can give them special attention.

The customer's name:

● ....

How I can give them special attention:

● I can ....

● I can ....

● I can ....

The customer's name:

● ....

How I can give them special attention:

● I can ....

● I can ....

● I can ....

MY MARKETING STYLE

People choose different ways to market their skills. Some choose to make contacts through friends, some choose to use advertisements, some choose to give free presentations, some choose to make cold calls. There is no right or wrong way. The only criterion is: Does it work? What is your preferred way of marketing?

My preferred marketing style is:

● To ....

....

....

● To ....

....

....

● To ....

....

....

MY NETWORK

Personal recommendation is the best advertisement and people often buy through networks. As a seller, how big is your network? Who do you know who might buy your products or services? Who do you know who has contacts? Draw a map of your personal network. Start with the people you know best, plus any customers, then expand your map. List everybody who might buy your products or put you in touch with potential customers:

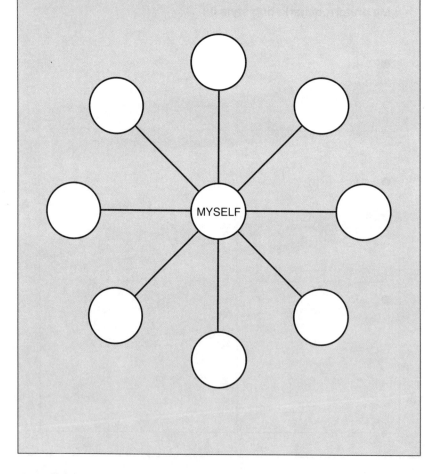

MY CUSTOMERS' WANTS

Make a list of all your customers and what each of these customers wants:

MY CUSTOMERS	WHAT THEY WANT
a)	● .... ● .... ● ....
b)	● .... ● .... ● ....
c)	● .... ● .... ● ....

MY CUSTOMERS' BUYING STYLE

Make a list of all your customers and how each of these customers buys things:

MY CUSTOMERS	HOW THEY BUY THINGS
a)	● .... ● .... ● ....
b)	● .... ● .... ● ....
c)	● .... ● .... ● ....

MY PRODUCTS:
The customer benefits

People buy things that they believe will improve their life or work. Why should people buy what you offer? What is in it for them? First: Describe the products and services that you offer to your customers. Second: Describe the benefits they will gain by buying these products and services. Be as specific as possible.

The products and services I offer to my customers are:

- ....

- ....

- ....

The benefits the customers will gain by buying these things are:

- They will ....

- They will ....

- They will ....

MY MARKETING CHANNELS

Bearing in mind how your customers buy things: What is the best way to reach them? Personal introduction, advertising, presentations, exhibitions or other methods? Whatever channel you use, how can you be distinctive and grab their attention? Describe the three best ways to reach your potential customers.

The three best ways to reach my potential customers are:

1) To ....

   ....

   ....

2) To ....

   ....

   ....

3) To ....

   ....

   ....

MY MARKETING PLAN

Building on what you have written, create your marketing plan. Bear these things in mind when making your plan: a) Your top customers. b) Your network. c) Your preferred marketing style. d) Your customers' wants. e) Your customers' buying style. f) Your products and the customer benefits. g) Your marketing channels. Be selective to be effective. Describe three specific things you can do to market what you offer and reach potential customers. Make sure you also build in some early successes.

My marketing plan is:

1) To ....

....

....

2) To ....

....

....

3) To ....

....

....

YOU CAN REACH YOUR GOALS

Dennis Potter, the playwright, recognised the value of finishing. Despite suffering from crippling illnesses, he penned plays such as *The Singing Detective*, *Blue Remembered Hills* and *Pennies From Heaven*. During the last year of his life he embarked on writing two plays. Variously described as cantankerous, brilliant and courageous, he displayed inner peace during his final months.

"Life is good," he reported, in a television interview with Melvyn Bragg a few weeks before his death. The apple blossom outside the window of his Ross-on-Wye home was the most beautiful blossom he had ever seen. He added: "My worst nightmare is to die four pages too early." Dennis returned home to achieve his vision. He died in May 1994, having completed his two final plays.

Everybody has a track record of finishing. People complete millions of tasks during their lives. They perform daily chores, cook meals, build houses, raise children, write reports, paint pictures or whatever. "But I hardly ever finish anything," protested Mark, a participant on a Career Development course. "I feel fired-up about an idea, set my goal and start working. Doubts begin to crowd my mind and I get diverted. My house is full of unfinished projects."

Peak Performers also start lots of projects and only complete a few. What is the difference? Pursuing their driving vision, they choose to be selective to be effective. Saying "Yes" to some things means saying "No" to others. Good finishers are totally single-minded. Keeping their eyes on the goal, they toil until they create visible results.

Finishing is a key part of life, but this highlights a paradox. People often finish best when they relax. Straining to reach a goal can be self-defeating. Linford Christie, the Olympic 100-metre Gold Medallist, devoted years to following his disciplined training schedule. He set his sights on winning specific competitions. Warming up properly before races, he got into the right rhythm.

Standing behind the starting line, he stared down the lane, looking beyond the finishing tape. Exploding out of the blocks, he sped down the track, using every muscle in his body. Twenty metres before the tape he switched into over-drive. Years of training paid off. Linford's inner discipline took over and he relaxed. He followed his flow, focused on the goal and kept going until he finished.

The next pages look at the art of finishing, but this must be seen in a wider context. Linford Christie and Dennis Potter had already done at least 80 per cent of the work. They spent years doing the right things in the right way to put themselves in an excellent position to achieve their goals. Getting the basics right became second nature. Such inner discipline paid off, especially when things got tough. Calling on years of inner wisdom, they coped with success and setbacks. They kept doing what worked, used their talents and produced positive results.

Assuming you have reached a similar stage in your work, how can you achieve your vision? Peak Performers often take three steps towards completing the creative process. They Flow, Focus and Finish. Let's explore how you can follow these steps in your own way.

You can Flow

Flow is the title of a pioneering book written by Mihaly Csikszentmihalyi. Building on Abraham Maslow's theory of peak experiences, he invited people to talk about the magical times when they felt fully alive. Artists, musicians and surgeons were the first to be interviewed. He then studied people from all over the world, such as factory workers in Chicago, farmers in Italy and teenagers in Tokyo. Happy times don't just happen, concluded Mihaly; people often make happiness happen. People create a sense of flow when:

1) They tackle a task which they have a chance of completing.
2) They concentrate on what they are doing.
3) They have clear goals.
4) They get immediate feedback.
5) They experience a deep and effortless involvement that removes the frustrations of everyday life.
6) They enjoy a sense of control over their actions.
7) They find their concern for self disappears, but paradoxically their sense of self emerges stronger.
8) They find the experience is so enjoyable that their sense of time disappears.

Flow is often a by-product that comes from immersing yourself in a meaningful activity. But this is not the whole story.

People can create a sense of flow when preparing to tackle a challenge. The athlete warms up before a race. The dancer practises at the barre before

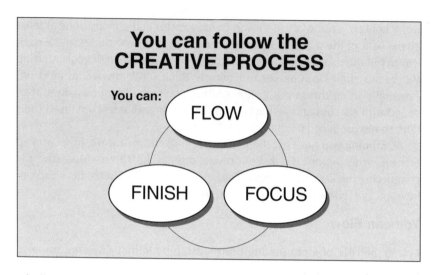

a ballet. The speaker prepares physically and mentally before delivering a speech. Taking a deep breath, they then step on to the stage. Buddhists meditate before starting their day. The author performs favourite rituals before putting pen to paper.

Embarking on a piece of writing, I set aside several days to prepare properly. The pages then begin to flow. Some writers create punchy prose at the drop of a hat, but I can't. Three or four weeks into the book, however, the words are emerging so quickly that sometimes I must slow down. People can cultivate the right rhythm to produce creative work.

How can you start flowing? Try tackling the following exercise called Flow. Different people do different things to get into their rhythm. They set aside a block of time, play favourite music, start the day with an early success, drink tea or whatever. Describe how you can keep your creative juices flowing. One way is to keep a daily journal called My Right Book. (See later page.) Develop the habit of writing: a) Three things I did right today. b) Two things I can do even better tomorrow. A good exercise for encouraging yourself, it nurtures two vital skills. First: To keep doing what works. Second: To keep improving. Practising such habits will keep your flow going. The next step is to fix your eyes on the goal.

You can Focus

Peak Performers concentrate on achieving a specific goal. Christina Noble focused on helping street children in Vietnam. Linford Christie focused on winning the Olympic Gold. Bob Geldof focused on raising money for Live Aid. "Get your hands into your pockets and send us your money," he yelled into the television cameras, haranguing his worldwide audience. Committed people are not easy companions. Some would call them "determined". Others would call them "stubborn", "obstinate" or "pig-headed".

A writer I know says: "Pinned on my studio wall is a picture of the books I want to complete in my life. Each day is a gift I am given to take a step towards completing this picture. Waking up in the morning, I lie still in bed for five minutes. In my mind's eye I look forward to the day ahead. I create a picture of the pages I want to complete during the next 12 hours. I then get up and begin my work for the day. If I ever get side-tracked, I look at the picture in my studio. My motto is: 'Keep the picture.' I soon get back on track."

FLOW

When do you feel most creative? When do you flow? How do you get your creative juices going? Different people do different things to get into their rhythm. They set aside a block of time, play music, start the day with a success, drink tea or whatever. Describe three concrete things you can do to ensure you continue to flow.

Three concrete things I can do to continue to Flow:

1) I can ....

....

....

2) I can ....

....

....

3) I can ....

....

....

MY RIGHT BOOK

Three things I did right today

- I ....

  ....

- I ....

  ....

- I ....

  ....

Two things I can do even better tomorrow

- I can ....

  ....

- I can ....

John Gaustad is somebody who focused on achieving a specific business vision. Walking around London in the early 1980s, he noted specialist bookstores devoted to stamps, religion, music, the occult, therapy, politics and the arts. John spotted a gap in the market which he would enjoy filling. Millions of British sports followers lacked their own bookstore. Sportspages opened its doors to customers in 1985. Situated just off Charing Cross Road, it has gone from strength to strength and, in 1992, opened a second shop in Manchester.

"Sounds an obvious idea," somebody may say, speaking with the benefit of hindsight. But a relevant question in the early 1980s was: "Do sports fans read?" Football fans were considered illiterate hooligans, for example, but John spotted a growing market. Articulate supporters were using desktop publishing to produce fanzines, many of which built cult followings.

Homesick Americans longed to read *Sports Illustrated* and other magazines devoted to American football, baseball, basketball and ice-hockey. Fans of athletics, golf, rugby and other sports scoured bookshops to read about their passion. Sportspages catered for all sports fans, providing a massive range of books, magazines, videos and sports memorabilia. John's idea worked because he brilliantly filled a specific niche in the market.

How do you channel your energies? Try tackling the exercise called Focus. Describe how you can concentrate on reaching a specific target. Peak Performers employ techniques such as visualising positive pictures. They picture the perfect result, the perfect audience, the perfect painting, the perfect book or the perfect finished product. They then work towards fulfilling this picture.

How can you keep your eyes on the goal? Try tackling the exercise My Finished Products. Draw a picture of the key things you want to do or create in your life. Put it somewhere where you see it every day. Keep focusing on the picture. Sounds odd, but you will start doing things that take you closer to achieving your target. Let's move on to the next step.

You can Finish

Finishing is often a by-product. Providing you keep doing the right things in the right way, finishing just happens. Achieving a vision is the result of following good habits. Like a ripe fruit falling from a tree, the final product simply appears one day. You can relax, celebrate and enjoy the fruits of success. Good finishers gain their greatest satisfaction, however, when they keep faith with their real mission in life.

"I finish lots of tasks at work, but I still feel something is missing," said one woman senior executive. "I am the world's best implementer. During the past ten years I have climbed the corporate ladder, but the long hours and macho culture have exacted a price. I am even thinking of leaving the company."

Many successful women, and some men, are doing the unthinkable, says Susan Wittig Albert in her book *Work Of Her Own*. Such people now see the next stage of Career Development to be Career Leaving. Why? Susan catalogues her own experiences in the corporate world. Rapid promotion led to her becoming vice-president of the company. But her personal life suffered. Two marriages collapsed and, feeling distant from both parents, she only visited them twice in five years. Three children left home to pursue their own lives. New relationships began in a guarded manner and were suddenly broken off. Sixty-hour weeks created stress, leading to back-aches and head-aches. Drinking, smoking and over-eating led to ill-health. She had

FOCUS

How do you focus? How do you channel your energy towards achieving a specific target? Peak Performers often picture the perfect finished product. They then work towards fulfilling this picture. How do you keep your eyes on the goal? Describe three concrete things you can do to ensure you continue to focus.

Three concrete things I can do to continue to Focus:

1) I can ....

....

....

2) I can ....

....

....

3) I can ....

....

....

MY FINISHED PRODUCTS

Draw a picture of the key things you want to do or create in your life. Put this picture in a place where you can see it every day. Providing you keep focusing on the picture, you will find that you start doing things that take you closer to fulfilling your picture.

no time for hobbies or meeting friends. Susan felt she was suffering from what the Jungian psychologist, June Singer, called "the sadness of the successful woman".

Susan took a year off to recapture her life. Earning enough money to pay the bills, she stopped living on credit. Spending more time at home, she ate better food, gave up alcohol and tobacco, and felt healthier. Writing about women Career Leavers, she found that sometimes the greatest resistance they face is from other women. "You are a good model for young women," is the argument. "If you leave, that will damage the cause of others in the company." Susan discovered, however, that many women are leaving the corporate world. Why?

- They want to re-connect with their feminine self.
- They are fed up playing masculine games. They also want to do things for themselves, rather than for the corporate culture.
- They want to pursue their own development, spending time with friends and pursuing activities other than work.
- They want to support themselves, however, and undertake rewarding work that also pays the mortgage.
- They want to recapture their enjoyment of life.

Career Leavers are showing fresh ways to live a healthy and happy life in our society, says Susan. Far from being anti-social, these people are the new pioneers. Money is initially perceived as a stumbling block, but they are learning how to live on less income. *Work Of Her Own* is a ground-breaking book. Passing on her wisdom, Susan shows how people can achieve a new vision of success. Finishing is a key skill, so it is vital to apply it to the real mission you want to pursue in your life.

Finishing also calls for daily discipline. Martha Graham, the American dancer, said that it takes ten years of daily training to hone the human body. Ten years of sweat to produce a dancer. Training must then become a daily habit for the remainder of their performing lives. Great performers do great things on great occasions. Why? Practice provides the foundation for them to make magic at the right moment. How can you do the right things in the right way every day? How can you complete your book, painting or other task? Try tackling the exercise called Finish. Describe three concrete things you can do to ensure you finish successfully. Nothing is guaranteed. But doing these things will increase the likelihood of achieving your vision.

FINISH

How can you keep doing the right things in the right way? How can you keep following your daily discipline? How can you overcome obstacles and keep working until you reach your goal? Describe three concrete things you can do to ensure you finish successfully.

Three concrete things I can do to finish successfully are:

1) I can

2) I can

3) I can

"Sounds plain sailing. What happens when you face tough times that throw you off course?" somebody may ask. Problems are often a symptom. They provide the opportunity for you to return to your values, reclarify your vision and practise good habits to produce visible results. People can grow stronger through overcoming setbacks. For example:

- Christina Noble overcame a traumatic childhood to help street children in Vietnam.
- Tamara Himmelstrand overcame peer pressure to conform and created new ways to help children to play the violin.
- Matt Busby overcame tragedy to rebuild Manchester United.
- Dennis Potter overcame painful illnesses to write memorable television plays.
- Alec Dickson overcame bureaucratic obstacles to create Voluntary Service Overseas and Community Service Volunteers.

Overcoming challenges to achieve your vision is a time for celebration. It is also a time for taking stock. "There's nothing more dangerous than yesterday's success" is an old saying. History is littered with the names of people, teams and companies that grew arrogant and fell from grace. Try tackling the following exercises which focus on the themes of learning from both successes and setbacks.

● Managing setbacks

Everybody has a track record of overcoming problems. First: Describe a setback in your life which you managed successfully. For example: failing an exam, losing a job or suffering rejection. Second: Describe five things you did right to overcome the setback. Third: Describe three concrete things you can do to manage setbacks in the future. The key is to maintain good habits, especially when times get tough.

● Managing success

People spend years exploring to discover the rich seam of success. Finding the seam is the start. They must then keep mining to gather the fruits of their labour. Some people make the mistake of walking away to start exploring elsewhere. Others become complacent, believing the hard part is over and everything will now fall into place.

This exercise is in three parts. First: Describe a time when you reached a goal and built on this achievement successfully. Second: Describe five things you did right to build on your achievement. Third: Describe three concrete things you can do to build on your achievements in the future. "Once you strike lucky, keep working", is a good motto for people who want to achieve ongoing success.

● **Celebrating success**

How can you commemorate your achievements? If you work alone, you may wish to buy yourself a present. If you work in a team, you may wish to have a party, give people awards, offer greater training opportunities, buy new equipment or introduce a profit share. Describe three concrete ways that you or your team can celebrate success. Rewarding achievements can generate energy and inspire people to tackle the next challenge.

MANAGING SETBACKS

1) Describe one setback in your life which you believe that you managed successfully.

● When I ....

....

2) Describe five things you did right to manage the setback successfully.

● I ....

● I ....

● I ....

● I ....

● I ....

3) How can you use what you learned? Describe three concrete things you can do to manage setbacks successfully in the future.

● I can ....

● I can ....

● I can ....

MANAGING SUCCESS

1) Describe a time in your life when you reached a goal and then built on this achievement successfully.

- When I ....

  ....

2) Describe five things you did right to build on your achievement successfully.

- I ....

- I ....

- I ....

- I ....

- I ....

3) How can you use what you learned? Describe three concrete things you can do to build on your achievements successfully in the future.

- I can ....

- I can ....

- I can ....

CELEBRATING SUCCESS

How can you commemorate your achievements? If you work by yourself, you may wish to buy yourself a present. If you work in a team, you may wish to have a party, give people awards, offer greater training opportunities, buy new equipment or introduce a profit share. What do you believe would be appropriate?

Three concrete ways I/we can celebrate success:

1) I/we can ....

....

....

2) I/we can ....

....

....

3) I/we can ....

....

....

You can pass on your wisdom to other people

Finishing is another name for beginning. Some people like to take a rest, other people grow restless. They start to clarify their next vision by asking themselves: "Should I do something similar or different?" Some pursue a similar path, others explore new fields. Everybody has skills, everybody has some form of wisdom, even if this is just knowing how to survive.

Who have been your great teachers? What lessons did they pass on to you? How did this improve your life? What knowledge can you pass on to other people? People often develop a sense of duty as they grow older. They feel an obligation to pass on their wisdom to future generations.

Adam Curle took this step in the 1960s. He has since spent 30 years acting as a mediator between warring factions in Europe, Africa and Asia. Reflecting back on the time when he graduated from university in the 1930s, he says: "I made myself a promise that I have kept, although somewhat laxly, never to work at anything that was not worthwhile." Adam then spent 25 years pursuing a distinguished career in education. Approaching the age of 50, however, he sought a greater purpose in life. Explaining the transition in his book *Tools For Transformation*, he writes:

"At that age I was still busy with my career which, after its late start, was going well. I had a chair at Harvard, was a fellow of the right learned societies, got invited to posh international conferences and to sit on important committees, had a nice home and a happy family: what else could anyone want? . . . But having fulfilled my professional ambitions, the whole academic circus began to pall. I started to refuse invitations unless they offered to pay my wife's expenses as well. I was ready for a change of gear."

Adam volunteered to mediate between conflicting parties in the Nigerian civil war from 1967 to 1970. He has since served in countries such as Pakistan, Zimbabwe, Northern Ireland, Afghanistan and Bangladesh. Mediators face similar tasks everywhere, says Adam, whether they are enabling the healing of pain in a marriage, a community or between nations. They must find ways:

- To reduce tension.
- To help opponents to stand back from fears and hatreds that have come to dominate their minds.
- To help opponents to see each other and their dispute more rationally in terms of what is of real interest to them and others involved.

- To help opponents to consider, however sceptically, the possibility of mending the relationship and becoming friends who can together strive to make the world more peaceful.

"This is when the process of mediation, as I have defined it, comes to an end," writes Adam. "Now the protagonists must talk to each other (perhaps with the help of a third party), negotiate, and discover themselves how to solve their joint problem. Above all, they must learn how to solve the problem *themselves*."

Mediators, negotiators and other peace makers aim to help others, but they must first learn to create peace within themselves, says Adam. Why? Imagine you are entering a room to face a general accused of war crimes. Your first job is to win his trust, which is impossible if you demonstrate prejudices, fear or hate. Adam practised meditation before meeting protagonists. Drawing on his Quaker and Buddhist ideals, he could then approach people with a loving heart. The peace maker's task is:

- To be a peaceful person.
- To build peaceful relations between people.
- To build peace-making conditions in the community, society and world.
- To show people the benefits of peace.
- To offer people models and tools which they can use to create ongoing peace.

"We must have some goal for the evolution of civilisation," said Adam, otherwise we stagger from crisis to crisis. Mediation can help by encouraging people to *"want to do the right things"*. (His italics.) Sounds a small step, but the results can be remarkable. The Biafran war ended in friendship, he recalls, and victorious solders helped the vanquished. Biafrans who had federal jobs before the fighting were quickly re-hired on full pay. Reconciliation was almost miraculous, says Adam, whose Biafran friends were deeply moved.

"Why did we do it?" they asked in amazed anguish, "What was it for? We lost a whole generation of our children for nothing. It was madness." Adam chose mediation as his way to encourage future generations.

People choose different ways to pass on their knowledge. Millions of "ordinary people" do so by being good parents, teaching students, training apprentices, demonstrating skills, telling stories, making films, painting pictures, inventing machines, staging exhibitions, acting as positive models, or whatever. Here are some well-known people who have passed on their wisdom.

- Jacqueline Du Pré, the cellist struck down by multiple sclerosis, passed on her knowledge by teaching students in master classes.

- Cicely Saunders, the founder of the modern hospice movement, passed on her knowledge by creating a model of caring for the dying at St. Christopher's Hospice in South London.

- Frank Lloyd Wright, the architect, passed on his knowledge by writing books, educating students and creating buildings.

- David Attenborough passed on his knowledge of nature by broadcasting wildlife television series, such as *Zoo Quest*, *The Living Planet* and *Life On Earth*.

- Antoine St. Exupery, the aviator, passed on his knowledge of flying and life by writing books such as *The Little Prince*, *Wind*, *Sand and Stars* and *Flight To Arras*.

- The Chipko Women's Movement, who saved forests in the Himalayas by hugging tree trunks and daring loggers to cut through them, passed on their knowledge by acting as inspiring models for people around the world.

- Martha Graham passed on her knowledge by teaching students and directing performances in her pioneering dance company.

How can you pass on your wisdom? As I mentioned earlier, everybody has gathered knowledge over the years, even if it is only knowing how to survive. Try tackling the exercise called Sharing My Wisdom. Describe how you can pass on your skills, knowledge and experience to people. Everybody can plant seeds of hope in their lives. Everybody can encourage both present and future generations, but don't expect instant results. Sometimes your flowers will grow tomorrow.

"My head is buzzing with ideas. When do we get on to action planning?" asked one person after one-and-a-half days on a Career Development workshop. You may be feeling something similar after reading this book. Soon we will move on to a final exercise looking at how to translate your values into action. But first a moment for reflection.

SHARING MY WISDOM

Everybody has skills. Everybody has gathered some form of wisdom during their lives, even if it is only knowing how to survive. Describe three concrete ways you can pass on your knowledge to other people. For example: being a good parent, teaching students, training apprentices, writing books, giving speeches, making films, inventing a machine, staging exhibitions, being a positive model, or whatever. Be as specific as possible.

Three concrete ways I can pass on my wisdom to other people are:

1) I can

2) I can

3) I can

CONCLUSION

People need a time for reflection. The old-style retreat provided such an oasis for the soul. Retiring from the world, you set aside your daily cares. Retreating into yourself, you became re-acquainted with your personal or spiritual life. Listening to the soul called for both calmness and courage. Why? It meant re-focusing on the important things in life. Sometimes the messages were challenging. Being true to your mission, for example, often called for making radical changes. "People create their own reality," says the Zen Master. So the next step was to rehearse how to manage the hurly-burly of daily life. Good intentions can soon get ambushed by mindless activity. Providing the re-entry was managed properly, you emerged feeling refreshed. You began to create a new reality in the outside world.

People need a time for reflection in the modern world. Like nature, they need a time for rest, renewal and rebirth. How do you renew yourself? Sleep, weekends, holidays, workshops and other "retreats" can provide this

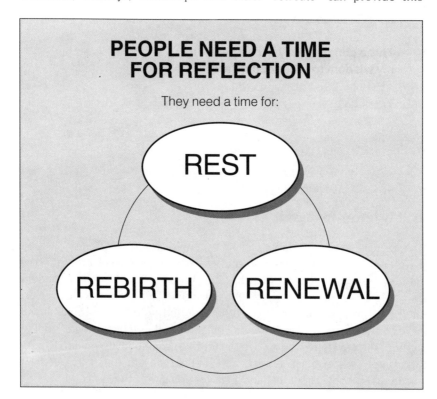

PEOPLE NEED A TIME FOR REFLECTION

They need a time for:

REST

REBIRTH

RENEWAL

opportunity. Otherwise people become hypnotised by the gods of speed, growth and profit. What happens if you do not take time to reflect? Illness is the body's way of telling us to slow down. Crises force us to take stock of our lives. Vulnerability is a great teacher. Sometimes we are shocked into getting the right balance between our mission and mortgage. Books can also provide a retreat. They offer a chance to reassess what is valuable in life. The following pages offer three final exercises on the theme of shaping your future life.

● My learning

Take a moment to reflect back over the pages. Describe three things you have learned or, more likely, have re-learned from reading the book. You can also adapt this exercise to help people clarify their learning from a workshop. "The Career Development course has provided tips which I can apply in my business," said one participant. "But the key lesson has been one of confirmation. I now believe I am travelling the right road in my life." You may have a similar feeling after reading this book. On the other hand, you may wish to pursue a radically different road in the future.

● My action plan

How can you build on your strengths, set specific goals and achieve success? Describe three concrete things you want to do in your work. "Will plus Skill can Thrill," say people in sports. Athletes must be ready to work hard before they can apply their skills and thrill the audience. How strong is your will? What is the likelihood of your doing each of the things you have written? Rate the probability out of 10. Start by tackling something where you have at least a 9 out of 10 chance of achieving success.

● My letter to myself

This exercise has been adapted by many people over the years. First: Take an envelope. Write your name and address on the front. Pick a date in the future, for example, in three months time. Write on the envelope: "To be sent on ....../....../......" Second: Write a letter to yourself. Start something like: "By the time I receive this letter I will have done the following things: I will have.........................." Describe what you aim to achieve by this date. Put the letter in the envelope. Third: Give the letter to somebody to mail to you on that date. This exercise is also an excellent way to finish a course. It encourages people to set realistic goals for doing work they love.

MY LEARNING

Take a moment to reflect and look back through the book. Follow this by describing:

Three things I have learned — or re-learned — reading the book:

1) I ....

....

....

2) I ....

....

....

3) I ....

....

....

MY ACTION PLAN

Write three specific things you want to do in your work. Then rate the probability — out of ten — of your doing each of these things.

I want:

1)   To ....

   ....

   The probability of my doing this is: . . . ./10

2)   To ....

   ....

   The probability of my doing this is: . . . ./10

3)   To ....

   ....

   The probability of my doing this is: . . . ./10

MY LETTER TO MYSELF

Date . . . .

To be posted to me in three months time on . . . . / . . . . / . . .

By the time I receive this letter I will have done the following things towards doing work I love:

1) I will ....

....

....

2) I will ....

....

....

3) I will ....

....

....

Yehudi Menuhin, the violinist, has dedicated his life to creating music. Speaking eloquently about the seduction of the studio, he says that rehearsals occupy years of the performing artist's time. But one day you must emerge from your retreat. One day you must step on stage to face your audience. Like falling in love, the journey is both frightening and beautiful. Writing in *The Best of Resurgence*, Yehudi explains:

"When I prepare a concert and finally walk on to the stage to make music, I too go out to meet my dream, my love, to substantiate it into living sound, the living message I have trained myself to create, and to achieve which I have dedicated many decades, for I share my world with an audience to whom my message and my premise are intelligible."

One day we must all emerge from our retreat. One day we must all step on stage to create our future reality. Everybody is an artist, everybody is creative, everybody can do work they love. Everybody can use their gifts to inspire future generations. *The Positive Workbook* cannot change people's lives. But it can offer tools which people can use to change their own lives.

Take the ideas you like best and use them to encourage yourself and other people. Blessed are those who have found their work, because they give the fruits of their talent to the world.

ACKNOWLEDGEMENTS

The author and publishers acknowledge with thanks permission to reproduce extracts from the following publications:

Arriving Where We Started edited by Michael Edwards. Copyright © 1983 by Voluntary Service Overseas and Intermediate Technology Publications, London.

The Best of Resurgence published by Green Books. Copyright © 1991 by Resurgence Ltd, Hartland, Devon.

Father of Football by David Miller, published by Stanley Paul & Co. Ltd., London. Copyright © 1970 by David Miller.

Making a Living Without a Job by Barbara Winter. Copyright © 1993 by Barbara Winter. Extracts used by permission of Bantam Books, a division of Bantam Doubleday Dell Publishing Group, Inc., New York.

Staying Sane in the Arts by Eric Maisel. Copyright © 1992 by Eric Maisel. Published by The Putnam Publishing Group, New York.

Tools for Transformation by Adam Curle. Copyright © 1990 by Adam Curle. Published by Hawthorn Press, Stroud, Gloucestershire.

Photograph: Philip Price

MIKE PEGG

Mike Pegg lives near Ross-on-Wye and has spent the past 30 years working as an Encourager. Leaving school at 15, he spent six years on a factory assembly line before Community Service Volunteers gave him the opportunity to help other people. He went on to run therapeutic communities for young people, qualifying as a psychotherapist and teaching family therapy.

During the 1970s he ran Encouragement Workshops throughout Europe, as a result of which he was invited to train business leaders, government decision-makers and national sports teams. He now works with TMI, a leading training consultancy company, specialising in helping people who want to achieve and maintain peak performance. His clients include Sony, Lunn Poly, Air Miles, the Dorchester Hotel and the Young President's Organisation.

FURTHER POSITIVE READING

Available through leading booksellers or from
the publisher's address shown:

THE ART OF ENCOURAGEMENT:
How You Can Encourage Yourself and Other People
by Mike Pegg (ISBN 0-9521358-1-7)

How can you encourage yourself? How can you encourage other people? How can you encourage people across the planet? This book is ideal for leaders, coaches, teachers and anybody who must inspire others to do their best. It is both positive and practical. It demonstrates how you can inspire people to achieve excellence in their lives and work.

Published in 1995 by Enhance Ltd,
The Hall, Radford Hall, Radford Semele,
Leamington Spa, Warwickshire,
CV31 1FH
Tel: 01926-431580. Fax: 01926 316749
£12.99 (postage and packing on application)

THE POSITIVE PLANET:
People Who Work to Build a Better World
by Mike Pegg (ISBN 0-9521358-0-9)

This book provides a hopeful vision. It shows how people can use their talents in their daily lives and work. People will shape the future whether they like it or not. The only question is whether they will do it for good or evil. This book offers practical ways for people to encourage future generations and build a better world.

Published in 1993 by Enhance Ltd,
The Hall, Radford Hall, Radford Semele,
Leamington Spa, Warwickshire,
CV31 1FH
Tel: 01926-431580. Fax: 01926 316749
£13.99 (postage and packing on application)